EMPIRE or REPUBLIC?

American Global Power and Domestic Decay

James Petras and Morris Morley

ROUTLEDGE   NEW YORK   LONDON

EMPIRE OR REPUBLIC?

Published in 1995 by

Routledge
29 West 35th Street
New York, NY 10001

Published in Great Britain by

Routledge
11 New Fetter Lane
London EC4P 4EE

Copyright © 1995 by Routledge

Printed in the United States of America on acid-free paper.

Library of Congress Cataloging-in-Publication Data

Petras, James F., 1937–
    Empire or republic? : American global power and domestic decay /
by James Petras, Morris Morley.
      p. cm.
    Includes index.
    ISBN 0-415-91064-1 (alk. paper) : —ISBN 0-415-91065-X (pbk. : alk. paper)
    1. United States—Politics and government—1993–   2. United
States—Politics and government—1981–1989. 3. United States—
Politics and government—1989–1993. 4. United States—Foreign
relations—1993–   5. United States—Foreign relations—1981–1989.
6. United States—Foreign relations—1989–1993.   I. Morley, Morris
H. II. Title.
E885.P48   1994
327.73—dc20
                                         94-17398
                                             CIP

TABLE OF CONTENTS

[There is] an idea afoot that America is in decline and we're in decline because we are engaged abroad. "Over-extended," the prophets of decline call it. These are false prophets.

U.S. Secretary of State George Shultz, January 1989

Now that you are the only superpower, you think you can dictate policy to your allies and make them obey.

Senior aide to French President
François Mitterrand, May 1992

Others assert that domestic needs preclude an active foreign policy. . . . But let's be clear. The alternative to American [global] leadership is not more security for our citizens but less.

President George Bush, December 1992

Rallying Americans to bear the costs and burdens of international engagement is no less important [than in the past]. But it is much more difficult [today]. For this reason, those who recognize the value of our leadership in the world should devote far more energy to making the case for sustained engagement abroad and less energy to debates over tactics.

U.S. National Security Council
Advisor Anthony Lake, September 1993

INTRODUCTION

In recent years, a wide-ranging debate has emerged about whether or not the United States is a declining world power. For some this is a myth, contradicted by the growth of American political, ideological, and military influence in the Third World, the collapse of the Soviet empire, continued successful military intervention abroad, and the resurgence of industrial, high-technology export sales. Others, most notably Paul Kennedy, have challenged this interpretation, citing the declining U.S. share of world trade, its growing indebtedness, spiralling budget and trade deficits, and lagging technological competitiveness.

This debate is inextricably linked to the question of what constitutes global hegemonic power in the specific context of the 1990s. According to Harvard political scientist Joseph Nye and former Reagan administration official Henry Nau, global power is largely defined by "political leadership and strategic vision," a sense of "national purpose," and the ability to hold sway in the world of "ideas." They dispute the notion of America's global economic slide and declining competitiveness since the 1970s as either a "myth" (Nau) or vastly exaggerated (Nye). They contend that the superiority and influence of the American system and American values will eventually transcend the setbacks brought on merely by individual policymakers' mistakes, and the absence of "ideas" and "national purpose" at the top. The magic of the free market will arrest any temporary erosion of economic competitiveness and reveal its decline to be a flight of fancy.[1]

To Joseph Nye, the massive U.S.-led military buildup in late 1990 to confront Saddam Hussein testified to America's global resurrection: "the Gulf crisis show[ed] our strength."[2] But does it make sense to apply the word "strength" to an exercise that initiated worldwide economic and financial dislocations? Moreover, the very fact that the White House was willing to project military power as a first resort is less an indication of strength than weakness. And would an "America ascendant" have needed to fly its emissaries around the world, hands outstretched, seeking donations to sustain this military display? Japan and (West) Germany nearly had to be bludgeoned to make acceptable contributions despite the fact that the former is six times and the latter three times more dependent on Middle East oil than the United States.

Years ago, when the U.S. government actively promoted its exporters and overseas investors in every corner of the globe (over and above its military adventures), "free trade" was the battle cry of an ascending empire's multinational corporations. Today, major American industries from automobiles to machine tools to computers have lost crucial market shares to Japanese and European traders strongly backed by their respective states. And the exuberant cries of earlier times have been replaced by the complaints of a declining power muttering about unfair competition and lost domestic markets.

Historically, ascending global powers have always been the locomotives of the world economy; they have carried lesser nations with them to greater economic achievements. Ephemeral military flourishes, such as Operation Desert Shield/Desert Storm, are no sign of a country's prowess—no remedy for global or national economic decline. Military strength is an increasingly less relevant indicator of hegemony in the marketplace-dominated world of the late twentieth century. It cannot translate into resurgent economic power. Hence the paradox of U.S. overseas adventures and national decline, of military power and economic weakness. How can a state that depends on transfers and loans from its own competitors to balance its trade and cover its budget deficits be described as an ascending world power?

Writers who equate projections of "will" and "voluntarism" with global revival deceive themselves as to the conditions for being competitive and hegemonic in the 1990s. By failing to examine the economic underpinnings of global power—the material foundations, structural orientation, and composition of capital—these imperial revivalists miss the way in which U.S. global power is declining. External projections of power in the absence of inner economic strength is a recipe for eroding competitiveness.

Much of this debate, however, including the most complex and nuanced arguments, has revolved around the external position of the United States. What has been neglected are the domestic foundations of global power and, more importantly, the relationship between domestic development and the ability of the U.S. to sustain its power abroad. In the past, the assumption common to conservatives, liberals, and Marxists alike was that global hegemony was a critical accompaniment of national prosperity. Whether framed in the jargon of free-trade regimes or in the language of Lenin's theory of imperialism, it was assumed that global power assured access to goods, markets, and a low-cost labor force that promoted prosperity at home.

There is, though, increasing reason to doubt the benign effects of U.S. global power on the domestic economy. The fundamental thesis of this study is that the pursuit of world dominance by the U.S. political and capitalist classes, whether in its current military-ideological form or on the basis of some new global economic framework, increasingly depends on the appropriation of domestic resources: the reprogramming of state funds from social programs to promoting overseas expansion; the lowering of domestic wages and living standards to sustain high rates of profitability and market share in the global arena; an elite-dominated political system that sustains externally oriented structures and shapes national policy priorities; a regressive tax structure that reconcentrates income at the top (in the hands of the global actors); and the creation of a two-tiered economy and society in which the majority are linked to decaying domestic institutions while a small privileged elite pursue their accumulation drives within the global networks.

Approaching the end of the twentieth century a new class structure has emerged in the United States with two axes: one anchored in the productive sector oriented toward the international market; the other in the nonproductive sector of the domestic economy. The principal protagonists of this class structure are the senior executives of multinational corporations (agricultural, commercial, industrial), and other major investment and financial institutions. Around these new centers of power is a restricted circle of "supporting casts": lawyers, accountants, consultants, academics, publicists, and their technical and administrative cadres. Today, to be national is to be at the margin of profits and balance sheets and distant from the key decisions that shape the major contours of U.S. society; to be national and tied to the local market is to be at the middle levels of power, struggling over limited resources, correcting the abuses and excesses of those at the top, and transmitting the new "adjustments" and cutbacks dictated by the new centers of power to those at the bottom.

The old division between owners of the means of production and wage earners is giving way to new divisions between the leading classes in the international and national economies, and between those classes commanding the paper economy versus those engaged in the domestic productive economy. At the top there has emerged a powerful, cohesive group of globally oriented leaders of corporations and financial and investment houses, as well as media and communications moguls; at the bottom, a growing army of downwardly mobile former industrial workers, part-time or temporary employees with few, if any, benefits, and the homeless. In between is a polarized middle: on the one hand, affluent, upwardly mobile professionals looking for the main chance in the financial and international circuits; on the other, public sector employees and wage workers anchored in the national economy, subject to downward wage pressures and budget cutbacks (reallocation of state resources), and increasingly vulnerable to corporate decisions to relocate plants overseas, pursue mergers, and shift health care costs to employees.

The relation between the dominant economic class and the political elites* is centered in the executive branch of government (including the Federal Reserve) which has largely eclipsed the power of Congress, relegating it to a marginal reactive role in the formation of new global policies. It is the executive branch that has accorded priority to creating the conditions for overseas corporate expansion, whether promoting the restoration of capitalism in the former Soviet Union, supporting free market authoritarianism in the Third World, or undermining regimes in Central America and southern Africa pursuing noncapitalist development models. The dominant class is linked to the executive through the interchange of personnel, ideological affinities as a condition for access to government, and structural integration—global political power is linked to global economic actors (and vice versa).

Insofar as the leading sectors of U.S. capital are international (realize profits overseas, etc.) the state has increasingly been shaped by the needs of this sector—through financing of campaigns and more profoundly by links between state institutions and the structures of capital.** Existing ideology, state institutions, and economic structures (all "international") shape the framework for political debate and political economic policy. Democratic and Republican Parties and their candidates for the presidency are financially and politically linked to "global actors." To break with these sectors of capital would require a profound rupture with the overall structure of the existing economic system provoking a major crisis. Local capital and labor have little or no leverage in reversing state policy, because the state has little or no leverage in reorienting capital inward or downward without profoundly affecting the organization and profit margins of international capital.

* Throughout the study, our use of the term "dominant class" refers to those individuals who control the key positions within the leading (U.S.) capitalist economic institutions; our use of the term "elite(s)" refers to specific capitalist sectors and key policymakers, and is used interchangeably to describe power configurations shaping (U.S.) global policy.
** Today, the U.S. "state" refers almost exclusively to the executive branch: it is overwhelmingly "international" in composition (nearly all of its members are drawn from the new centers of power, independent of party affiliation), outlook, and, most important, in allocating societal and economic resources.

To the extent that the "state" or executive branch watch over domestic society, it has increasingly adopted the role of "enforcer," policing violence and discontent of those excluded from the new axis of economic activity. For the globally oriented elite, maintaining the practice of diverting state resources and confronting the consequences is basically a political problem: building "police barriers" so that the disorganization and crime spawned by the two-tiered system does not spill over into their work sites or lifestyles; containing domestic social expenditures so that they don't impinge on the state's ability to bail out capitalist sectors in crisis (e.g., financial institutions); ensuring a docile and politically impotent labor movement that poses no threat to the capacity of this elite to increase profits locally and appropriate home state resources in order to maximize expansion in the global political economy; and fostering competition among the have-nots in the national economy over dwindling resources by politicizing ethnic and racial divisions (up to a point).

In his influential book, *The Rise and Fall of the Great Powers*,[3] Paul Kennedy argues that excessive military spending and imperial "overreach" contributed to the U.S. global economic decline. This study contends that Kennedy overstates one factor (military spending) and underestimates the significance of the internationalization of capital. Moreover, he ignores the impact of the drive for global leadership on the national economy, domestic classes, and the welfare state; the increasing diversion of domestic resources overseas to compensate for stagnation and economic decline brought about by large-scale military spending, the rise of speculative capital; and the rapid growth of multinational (transnational) capital.[*] Our analysis also indicates that economic decline is confined to particular capitalist sectors—excluding U.S. multinational capital. Unlike Kennedy who warns of the danger to the entire U.S. system posed by the deterioration of the national economy, we stress the importance of identifying specific units and levels of analysis in talking about

[*] We use the terms "multinational" (MNC) and "transnational" (TNC) interchangeably.

"America's decline." We further argue that domestic decay is precisely the condition for the growth of power and wealth of international political and economic actors. As the empire expands the republic declines.

Other writers such as Seymour Melman have made a persuasive case for believing that the permanent war economy (militarism) was the major domestic factor that dulled America's competitive reflexes.[4] While we do not disagree with this argument, our study offers a more nuanced explanation that includes a focus on the diversion of capital to nonproductive investment at home and productive investment abroad. Furthermore, our analysis does not point to a general decline but to a more complex mosaic: the experiences of different sectors of the American economy vary (some expand, some decline, others register little change). Our thesis also takes issue with Paul Sweezy and Harry Magdoff who argue in their writings that American capitalism entered a phase of stagnation in the 1930s and only World War II and the subsequent Cold War militarization of the economy prevented its otherwise imminent collapse.[5] In today's United States, however, we show that capital growth (externally and internally) is no longer compatible with the welfare state, expanding social services, stable and well-paid jobs, etc. The central issue is not stagnation but the existence of a capitalist economy in the 1990s where recovery and growth is being accompanied by declining wages, massive job losses in the manufacturing sector, and cutbacks in social budgets.

This study addresses the class and institutionally specific features of the debate over America's "decline" or "ascendancy." Empire is not for everybody . . . nor is decline a condition that equally affects all economic sectors and classes. We focus on the uneven growth of the U.S. empire, its political and military dimensions, the transformations in U.S. capital (internally and externally), and the efforts to sustain global leadership by diverting resources from the domestic economy.

In summary, this book argues that understanding the debate about America's global position requires making two basic distinctions: one between political, military-ideological, and economic power;

the other between domestic and overseas class and state actors. On the basis of these distinctions we propose a number of theses about U.S. global power. First, that the U.S. is an ascending military, political, and ideological power. Second, that the U.S. national economy is declining relative to global competitors. Third, that U.S. multinationals are growing relative to the domestic economy. Fourth, and most important, as the empire grows by diverting domestic resources to sustain global power, the national economy and society deteriorates.

A NOTE ON THE CHANGING NATURE OF U.S. CAPITAL

Over the past decade or more two major shifts have occurred in U.S. capital: from the predominance of industrial to nonindustrial (financial, real estate, insurance, mass media, etc.); and from the predominance of domestic to overseas productive investment.

We identify three sets of capitalists: *finance capital* (those sectors related to nonindustrial capital) that operates at both the national/domestic and international levels; *international industrial capital* (multinational corporations being the prime unit) that "originates" in the United States but increasingly invests and produces in the global market; and *domestic capital* that produces goods and services in/for the U.S. market.

International capital seeks to realize profits abroad based on lower labor costs, and to shape state policy in order to facilitate the transfer of capital upward, open up new overseas markets, and create expanding investment opportunities abroad. To a considerable degree, the goals of finance capital overlap with those of international capital. It favors an activist state that deregulates the local economy, keeps interest rates low, opens up new international markets and investment opportunites, supports debt payments and debt swaps, etc. We refer to the financial capitalist class as having a parasitical relationship with the domestic economy because its earnings are not based on the production of goods and services but rather on the buying, selling, and stripping of productive enterprises and land.

National or "domestic capital" favors a state that acts to lower labor costs while opposing free markets and higher taxes to bail out losses sustained by finance capital, or subsidize mergers or imports of overseas competitors. Unlike the other two capitals, domestic productive capital is subject to trade union pressures, pays taxes, and can be harnessed to social welfare programs.

It is not that we "favor" productive over parasitic capital. Our argument is that one type produces useful goods while the other penalizes both workers and productive capital. In any event, capital moves between the productive and the parasitic. Theoretically, we would support productive over financial capital (if it were possible to distinguish) and within productive capital, workers' welfare over profits. Is it possible to reorient capital toward domestic production—expansion based on the local market and social welfare? Theoretically maybe, but practically unlikely.

1

REVIVING THE WORLD OF THE 1950s? THE U.S. AND ASCENDING GLOBAL POWER IN THE 1990s

The disintegration of the Soviet Union and its empire, European cooperation in the U.S.-orchestrated military intervention in the Gulf, the embrace by many Third World regimes of pro-U.S. economic and foreign policy positions, and Washington's aggressive pursuit of free-trade agreements that expand the scope of U.S. market penetration and political influence, are all powerful indicators of the renewed ascendancy of the U.S. in global politics. In this chapter, we discuss these and other relevant factors but simultaneously argue that Washington's capacity to exploit and turn them into long-term conditions for global ascendancy depends on the strength (political, economic, military, ideological) of its imperial institutions. Also highlighted is the emphasis in U.S. strategy on bolstering its ability to compete with new imperial rivals—Europe and Japan. Insofar as we consider the issue of whether the United States is a declining or rising political power, the major focus is on one aspect of this debate: the forces and events propelling global ascendancy.

PROJECTING AMERICAN POWER: A "NEW-OLD" WORLD ORDER

Since the early 1980s, the U.S. has wielded unprecedented political, military, and ideological power at the global level. In the military realm, the U.S. is de facto the world's only nuclear superpower. NATO has received a new lease; its functions have been extended to "policing" non-European regions and intervening in intra-European conflicts. Washington intervenes in Africa and the Middle East with impunity. It has been equally successful in promoting electoral transitions in Latin America and Asia (Philippines) that preserve the coercive institutions of existing states—thus retaining the allegiances of strategic clients. Moreover, under the aegis of "fighting the drug war," the Pentagon has established military bases and garrisons in the South American heartland that provide the wherewithal for directly intervening on the side of client regimes in their conflicts with guerrillas, peasant organizations, or popular movements. Indeed, several governments, notably those of Peru, Bolivia, and Colombia, have accepted the principle of a permanent U.S. military presence, ostensibly to eliminate the major sources of cocaine and other narcotics production—in the process severely compromising their national sovereignty. Last, but not least, the Reagan/Bush use of military force to solve perceived political problems, especially in Central America and the Caribbean, provoked only token regional opposition, in effect amounting to tacit complicity in these unilateral interventions in the internal affairs of supposedly independent states.

This era of prolonged counterrevolution—both cause and consequence of the revival of U.S. global power—also found expression in the ascendancy of Washington-sponsored, neo-liberal, economic doctrines as well as the subordination of former adversary regimes to the imperial state's political tutelage. This resurgent hegemony went hand in hand with declining living standards in target regions as newly elected clients rushed headlong to implement the free-market, deregulated policies favored by the Reagan and Bush administrations. In Latin America, for instance, the so-called lost decade of the 1980s was a catastrophe for the region's population: wages, employment, health, education, and other indices of living standards plummeted as the numbers falling below the poverty line reached historically high levels. But for American investors, traders, and bankers this was an era of booming profits in the hemisphere: over $200 billion in principal and interest payments flowed into the coffers of U.S. private banks while part of region's debt was converted into the takeover of profitable domestic assets at bargain basement prices; previously closed markets were opened up by the democratic, neo-liberal regimes to U.S. commerce; public enterprises were privatized and sold off at less than their true current value; and U.S. corporate investors moved south to take advantage of cheap labor, especially in Central America and the Caribbean.

In Latin America, Washington has never had an alignment of political regimes so favorable to its economic agenda or so desirous of establishing "stronger links" with the region's hegemonic power.[1] Neo-liberal policies, freeing markets, and the opening up of resource exploitation to foreign investors are the order of the day throughout the continent; labor costs have declined and national regulations and social legislation is at its weakest in over half a century. The transfer of lucrative public firms to overseas multinational enterprises and private banking through debt swaps and an accelerated privatization process is dramatically changing the balance of power between national and foreign capital, between public and private enterprise. In Canada and Mexico, free-trade agreements have opened up huge unfettered markets for American goods and financial services while deepening imperial investors' access to a huge labor market. The governments of Brian Mulroney and Carlos Salinas, and the export elites that supported them, accommodated Washington's desire to expand exports and appropriate national resources historically subject to public sector regulation.

In return for opening up their economies and markets, these countries were promised reciprocity in the form of equivalent U.S. concessions regarding market access and new large-scale inflows of development capital. The reality has been otherwise: having deregulated their economies at Washington's bidding, these U.S. clients, except Mexico, have been denied much in the way of new capital resources or market opportunities. Reciprocity has been subordinated to short-term profits and economic pillage that is perceived by U.S. officials as a springboard for regaining global economic power; through regional bloc advantages, Washington hopes to offset its competitive economic disadvantages vis-a-vis Japan and Germany.

Successful U.S. military interventions also hastened the expansion of ideological hegemony as adjoining states buckled under and

3

"redefined" the parameters of their action. In the ideological-cultural realm, U.S. success can be measured by the diminished influence of Marxist and nationalist ideologies and the increasing circulation of its own hegemonic formulas: in Latin America, interdependency and integration replaced imperialism and dependence; social contracts (concertación) substituted for class conflicts; "democracy" characterized elitist technocratic regimes cohabiting with terrorist state institutions and their death-squad allies. Many Latin intellectuals embraced free trade, regional integration schemes, debt payments, and debt swaps as the new "realism" and "pragmatism." Further testifying to the ascendancy of U.S. cultural hegemony in the region was the incorporation of many former leftist intellectuals into the neo-liberal governments, readily articulating the case for closer working relations with the dominant imperial power.

At the juridical level, the United States has codified its capacity to project power and act with impunity by declaring that American laws have international jurisdiction (the doctrine of "extraterritoriality"). Between 1987 and 1990, U.S. political, economic, and military warfare against Panama systematically violated international law.[2] This adherence to the doctrine of "extraterritoriality" culminated in the arrest, extradition (despite the absence of any bilateral treaty), and trial of Panamanian head of state, General Manuel Noriega. In June 1992, the U.S. Supreme Court affirmed that Washington had no obligation to respect international law and established extradition treaties. In a case involving a Mexican doctor spirited to the United States by American agents, it ruled that it was perfectly legal to kidnap criminal suspects from foreign countries for trial in the imperial state.[3] This decision gives virtually unlimited authority to U.S. intelligence agencies and armed forces around the world to apprehend the national of any country if Washington deems such action necessary. Later the same year, President Bush signed into law a bill making it illegal for overseas subsidiaries of U.S. multinationals to trade with Cuba—once more showing a total disregard for national sovereignty.

In the Middle East, the United States displayed the full range of its global political and military power: it intervened with unprecedented force against a local adversary (Iraq), in the process defining the nature of the political debate and creating new alliances. Formerly described "terrorist" states (Iran, Syria) cooperated in the war against Saddam Hussein; allied armies agreed to fight under American leadership; allied governments agreed to fund a large part of the war effort; the Soviet Union lined up behind Washington following the unceremonious rejection of its plan for a negotiated settlement of the conflict. The U.S. air war (saturation bombing) maximized the visibility of the imperial state, assured the loyalty of regional clients, and emphasized both the capacity and willingness of the Bush administration to use weapons of mass destruction to instill fear into, and intimidate, would-be enemies—backed by a pliant United Nations that had succumbed to White House pressure to legitimate the use of overwhelming force against Iraq. In a thinly veiled threat to replicate this projection of military power if deemed necessary in the future, President Bush repeatedly stressed America's responsibility for maintaining global stability.

The U.S. war in the Persian Gulf was an attempt to reaffirm Washington's role as global policeman; to resubordinate economic competitors (Japan, Europe) to military power; to convert rising economic hegemons into docile bankers of U.S. military conquests; to disaggregate European alliances in favor of U.S.-centered coalitions; to both trade Third World debt payments for agreement to participate in the U.S.-commanded multinational military force and simultaneously intimidate the Third World into submission. The extraordinary military buildup, the pressure on clients, allies, and neutrals to collaborate, the vast economic expenditures, and the intensity of the air war was, in its most profound sense, an attempt to change the rules of global power, to reverse all of the world historic trends that were relegating the United States to the status of a second-class hegemon. The war was meant to define a new military-centered global order in which markets, income, and resource shares were defined not by technological-market power but by political-military dominance. Under these rules, Washington's global supremacy would be assured.

The Gulf War was the culmination of a series of political and military victories that bolstered the U.S. global position: the reversal of revolutionary and nationalist regimes in southern Africa, Central America, and Asia; the creation of a new, pro-U.S. coalition including Russia, China, and a cluster of Arab and previously "neutral" Third World states; the steady disintegration of the nonaligned movement which signalled the end of calls for a New International Economic Order to be replaced by Washington's announcement of a New World Order; and a United Nations increasingly receptive to U.S. wishes. One Security Council diplomat characterized Bush administration pressure on the members of the international body to vote with it during 1991-92 as "more forceful than ever."[4]

U.S. global power received an enormous boost as a consequence of the disintegration of the Soviet Union and its empire in Eastern Europe. First, these developments have eliminated any significant counterweight to U.S. hegemonic aspirations; the United States can now project its power into most areas of the world without having to calculate the effects of a superpower response. Second, given Washington's new ability to act unilaterally, regimes seeking to pursue alternative economic and political strategies now face substantially increased costs in terms of both U.S. hostility and having to depend more on internal resources to defend and implement such programs. The result has been a tendency to reshape political and economic agendas to accommodate U.S. concerns, thus effectively acknowledging its hegemonic power. Third, Washington's position of strength is manifested in the new Russian elite's acceptance of U.S.-designed political and economic "reforms"—capturing the quasi-clientele relationship that has emerged. Fourth, Eastern Europe has also subordinated itself to U.S. hegemonic influence. Its new rulers, seeking to curry favor even when it adversely affects longstanding economic interests, have petitioned to join the U.S.-dominated NATO alliance, supported U.S. military initiatives in the Near East, implemented IMF austerity reforms in return for promised economic assistance, and ruptured a number of preexisting trade ties with Cuba. The region's willingness to adhere to the trade boycott with Iraq was perhaps most emblematic of this preparedness to make economic sacrifices in order to achieve "loyal follower" status in the U.S.-centered New World Order.

In addition to its growing global political and military power, Washington's ideological influence has never been stronger. One measure of its hegemony in this sphere is its capacity to secure large-scale support for its human rights double bookkeeping: the support for political purges of state institutions in Eastern Europe and the protection of longstanding military and police allies in Latin America. In the East, the rhetoric of unregulated capitalism ("free markets") has gained support from the great majority of intellectuals and the mass media. Such uncritical worship of U.S. imperial supremacy coincides with the idealization of authoritarian prerevolutionary elites and the obliteration and/or falsification of the intervening complex and contradictory histories of these countries. In the South, imperial investment and market takeovers have been described as "interdependence" and "integration," though the movements of capital are practically unidirectional.

American consumer patterns, cultural habits, and expressions increasingly displace national productions: in films and theater, videos, newspapers, radio, and advertisements, nationally oriented producers are left out and glossy, violent, sexually explicit, mindless mass production has gained sway. Interpretations of past histories, assessments of previous nationalist regimes' socioeconomic experiments reflect the same one-sided doctrinairism of Western academic ideologues. This projection of U.S. ideological hegemony in the East and South testifies to its new global authority—in a world where there are few effective competitors.

THE STRUCTURES OF AMERICAN GLOBAL POWER

Anchoring the growth of U.S. hegemony on a world scale is a structure of power built around interrelated sets of institutions: a military, navy, and airforce with far reaching interventionary capacity; extensive clandestine intelligence networks capable of undermining adversaries and bolstering clients; an enormous array of public and private mass media outlets around the world capable of projecting American definitions of international political and economic reality; and multiple collaborator classes, especially in the Third World, linked to informal (private) and formal (public) U.S. institutions. These components of U.S. global power are mutually reinforcing and their cumulative impact over time has far exceeded their separate activities in promoting and reinforcing U.S. aspirations abroad. Dependent on the U.S. state's ability to channel resources from the domestic economy and the national budget, these institutions underpinning American hegemony worldwide need to continually create those opportune moments and political rhetoric that justify their actions and the diversion of resources from the national economy.

In order to reconstruct the U.S. global military/clandestine apparatus in the post-Vietnam period, it rapidly became clear to American policymakers that this goal could only be accomplished by diverting public attention from "low politics" serving domestic social needs to the "high politics" of the state's international "responsibilities." In the late 1970s, the Carter administration's decision to jettison its human rights emphasis in favor of a renewed global covert and military buildup was justified by growing unrest and instability in the Third World, especially in the Middle East, the so-called hostage crisis in Iran and, most importantly, the Soviet invasion of Afghanistan. This shift toward a more interventionary foreign policy was taken over and vastly expanded by a Republican-dominated White House during the 1980s: military spending and CIA action programs around the world rose to unprecedented levels, facilitated by White House demonizing of heads of government viewed as hostile to U.S. imperial interests, particularly in Central America and the Middle East.

Over the past three decades, U.S. military spending has been on an accelerated upward spiral: during the Kennedy-Johnson years, it averaged $59 billion (in current dollars) yearly; under Nixon and Ford, the figure jumped to almost $82 billion; the much-lauded human rights administration of Jimmy Carter pushed it to $113 billion annually between 1977 and 1980; with the advent of the Reagan presidency, defense outlays skyrocketed past $240 billion annually.[5] This trend showed no sign of slackening off during the Bush presidency: over the four-year period, total spending exceeded $1.2 trillion.[6] The greatest absolute increases occurred at a time when the world's only other superpower was disintegrating, thereby reinforcing Washington's capacity and will to intervene in any region of the globe where imperial policy dictated.

As former National Security Council Advisor Zbigniew Brzezinski publicly boasted, the purpose of the U.S.-accelerated arms race in the late 1970s and 1980s was not in response to any Soviet threat. Rather, it was an effort to force Moscow to divert resources to the military sector and thereby provoke a combined economic and political crisis—an outcome that Washington ultimately succeeded in achieving.

U.S. military spending during the Reagan-Bush era captures perfectly the contrast between Washington's unproductive preoccupations and those of Tokyo, Bonn, and other European capitals. While Pentagon outlays rose from $144 billion in 1980 to $286 billion in 1990 (in constant 1987 dollars), Germany's budget increased from $28 billion to $36 billion and Japan's from $11 billion to $29 billion. The contrast is even more striking if military spending is calculated as a percentage of each country's Gross National Product (GNP): in 1986, the figures were 6.7%, 3.1%, and 1.5% for the United States, Germany, and Japan respectively; by 1992, while the percentage gap between the United States and Germany remained virtually unchanged, it had actually widened between the United States and Japan.[7] Instead of indulging in unprecedented levels of military spending, America's major competitor allies focused their energies and resources on developing strategic industrial sectors and expanding global trade to bolster their economies—literally at Washington's expense.

The need to deal with continuing "danger points" in the Third World remained one of the primary justifications offered by U.S. policymakers for maintaining large military and intelligence budgets in the post-Cold War era. In late 1990, the U.S. Defense Secretary

Richard Cheney observed: "The best way to maintain the peace is to be prepared for war and the 'peace dividend' is peace and it's worth every penny we paid for it."[8] For the Third World, such Orwellian language ("war is peace") could reasonably be translated as "self-determination is U.S. intervention."

Covert political and military activities were perhaps the fastest growing sectors of the U.S. government during the 1980s. By 1989, the President's so-called black budget that funded the secret wars against established, internationally recognized governments in Central America, southern Africa, and Afghanistan had grown to an astronomical $36 billion a year.[9]

The intelligence apparatus of the American state is composed of 13 spy agencies with a collective 1992 budget estimated at more than $29 billion. Over 50% of funds allocated for intelligence collection and analysis since the Truman era has been absorbed in monitoring of the Soviet bloc countries.[10] For instance, the primary task of the National Security Agency, which receives the largest percentage of the intelligence budget, was to decode communications between Soviet political and military leaders. But the end of the Cold War and the disappearance of the Soviet "threat" has not resulted in a lowered profile or major spending cuts in spying agency budgets. Rather, there has been a shift to new areas of concentration and new styles of intervention. "We will have almost no concerns about military activity in Eastern Europe," observed Bobby Ray Inman, the former head of the National Security Agency, "but we will be vastly more interested in internal stability, economic and political developments. It's not that we are going to be doing vastly less, but we're going to be doing it in the open."[11] Instead of a reduction in CIA staff numbers, employees have been moved in accord with the reordered priorities: one-third of the covert agency's military analysts are now working in "other areas of the agency."[12]

During the latter part of the Bush administration, a number of proposals were floated within the intelligence community and the U.S. Congress on the need for a much greater involvement by the CIA in activities designed to increase America's economic competitiveness abroad. Some advocated spying on allies and trading partners, including purloining of business secrets that might be helpful to U.S. corporations. According to former CIA head Admiral Stansfield Turner, "We steal secrets for our military preparedness. I don't see why we shouldn't to stay economically competitive." Others, such as the chairman of the Senate Intelligence Committee David Boren, argued for a crackdown on foreign economic espionage. Robert Gates, Reagan's deputy director of the CIA and Bush's director, proposed more extensive monitoring of "collusion" between foreign governments and their overseas capitalists that "harm" American multinationals and an active program involving the CIA and the FBI to safeguard U.S. trade secrets.[13]

Rising worldwide military and clandestine capacity was paralleled by a similarly dramatic increase in funding of the state's ideological (and cultural) organizations that were charged with responsibility for "selling" and legitimating the interventionist foreign policy. The United States Information Agency (USIA) budget, for instance, increased from $300 million in 1981 to over $1 billion in 1989.[14] This domestic and worldwide mass media apparatus placed itself at the service of the Reagan/Bush White House, saturating the print and visual outlets with demonological images of political targets as drug dealers (Noriega) or Hitlerian figures (Hussein), and providing the moral rationales to support imperial military, economic, and covert warfare. To sell these projections of power into the Third World, new propaganda agencies were also established. They included the Office of Public Diplomacy which was part of a massive propaganda-psychological campaign to win support for U.S. Central American policy at home and abroad.[15] The ability of the U.S. to transmit its moralizing propaganda around the globe was the accompaniment to its new interventionism—the toppling of "unacceptable" governments and the imposition of client regimes.

The projections of U.S. military and ideological power also depend on the existence of collaborator classes in target nations for maximum impact. Between the late 1940s and the mid-1970s, Washington cultivated and recruited Third World military officials, traditional oligarchies, and rising industrialists who viewed the world in the image of U.S. interests. Since the late 1970s, the imperial state has increasingly wooed that class of upwardly mobile professionals and intellectuals tuned into the neo-liberal economic rhetoric, addicted to the consumer society and frustrated by the constraints of egalitarian ideology and limits on individual expression. The targeting of this group derived from their profound addiction to Western living standards and their craving for acceptance as part of "Western civilization."

The crucial role these educated classes played was in fashioning the symbols, movements, and ideology of modernity, interpreted as "breaking with the past" and opening up their economies and societies to the West. While the U.S. mass media projected an image of these individuals, whether in Latin America, Asia, or Eastern Europe, as independent-minded democrats linking free markets and foreign investment with modernity, their actual role was to act as intermediaries translating Western interests into symbols of modernization. This meant disintegrating the old units of power (Communist Parties, nationalist parties, overseas alliances) and then reconnecting with the existing Western centers of power in a dependent relationship—offering lucrative concessions in exchange for privileged positions within the new international hierarchy.

Through large-scale, long-term funding of "private foundations" and various forms of covert assistance, the U.S. consolidated the ideological affinities of these intermediary or compradore classes. When they came into conflict with local authorities, whether dictators in the South or bureaucrats in the East, Washington provided them with visibility and, on occasion, exerted its influence to neutralize a repressive response and enhance their "leadership" qualities. The successful meshing of U.S. external projections of power and the ascendancy of these educated classes in East and South were decisive in shifting the balance of global power in favor of the United States.

Ironically, though, the United States has shown little capacity to economically sustain its new allies in government. Washington's military and ideological institutions—the basis of its global power—depend upon the state's capacity to continually divert resources from the domestic economy to sustain overseas expansion, a source that is shrinking and increasingly difficult to tap. In the case of Latin America, the Bush administration's incapacity to rebuild economically viable client states was demonstrated by its "trade not aid" formula that lacked any strategic commitment to large-scale, long-term investments to expand productive capacity.[16] Eastern Europe fared no better. During 1990 and 1991, the United States committed a merely $5.75 billion in aid to the former Soviet bloc countries compared to $80 billion in pledges from the European Community (most from Germany).[17] The economic crises, South and East, triggered by the application of U.S. ideological prescriptions left these educated classes in government floundering and desperately seeking foreign assistance, primarily from non-American sources.

WASHINGTON'S STRATEGY FOR GLOBAL DOMINATION

Ever since the first cracks and fissures began to appear in the Soviet Union's hold on superpower status during the Gorbachev era, senior U.S. foreign policymakers have exhibited a striking lack of realism about America's capacity for policing the world. They decried the "false prophets of global decline,"[18] and notwithstanding the new authority of Europe and Japan, continued to insist that the United States must not abandon its hegemonic position within the Western world. In September 1989, Deputy Secretary of State Lawrence Eagleburger told a Georgetown University audience that it was incumbent on the United States "to take the lead in safeguarding and expanding the institutional mechanisms which are vital to the preservation of international economic and political stability. Our capacity to play this role may have been diminished, but the need for us to do so has not."[19]

In the aftermath of the Soviet bloc's collapse into competing fragments with economies in decay, Washington's "belief in its own myths," its dream of forging a strategy to insure unchallenged U.S. global hegemony, strengthened considerably. Since then, it has been revealed as one of the worst kept secrets in post-Cold War interstate politics. It was at the very center of the U.S.-orchestrated military intervention in the Persian Gulf in late 1990; it underpinned the Bush White House efforts to maintain a belligerent posture toward the defeated Iraqi regime of Saddam Hussein, to incite trade conflicts with Japan, to accelerate the free-trade agreements strategy with countries to its north and south, to oppose any significant moves to cut exorbitantly high U.S. levels of military spending, and to pressure European allies to accept a continuing high profile for NATO.

Global domination essentially involves a large network of client regimes subservient to America's interests in the Third World who open their markets to U.S. exports, promote and protect U.S. investors and allow them access to raw materials, and who follow White House leadership on regional and international issues. For the advanced capitalist countries, U.S. domination means the elaboration of policies to discourage them from challenging or displacing U.S. economic, political, and military interests in any part of the world.

The most systematic and explicit statement of the strategy of U.S. global dominance was formulated in a February 1992 document ("Defense Planning Guidance for the Fiscal Year 1994–1999")[20] prepared by an interagency collaboration between the State Department and the Pentagon, in conjunction with the National Security Council and in consultation with the president and his senior foreign policy advisors. The document was not the expression of personal opinions of low-level officials seeking to influence the higher-ups; rather, it was a basic guide to the strategic thinking among the most influential agencies and officials of the foreign policy apparatus. An analysis of the Defense Planning Guidance (DPG) and Bush global strategy reveals a great deal about the basis, organizational instruments, and objectives of American power abroad.

The collapse of the Soviet Union and the disintegration of its Eastern European empire, together with the military victory over Iraq, are described in the DPG as offering unique opportunities for resurgent global empire building. These "two victories" have created a "new international environment," reaffirmed "U.S. global leadership" and "integrat[ed]" (i.e., subordinated) competitor allies Germany and Japan into a "collective security" system under U.S.

leadership.[21] They constituted in the minds of Bush policymakers a powerful stimulus to Washington's expansionist impulse; they did not prefigure, as Gorbachevian "new thinkers" and numerous American liberal and conservative analysts asserted, a lessening of it.

The global pretensions derived from such political and military victories were largely based on Washington's capacity to project military power. To insure that this didn't change, the DPG proposed that the White House fund a 1.6 million military force over the next five years at a cost of $1.2 trillion in order to sustain America's role as global policeman.

The DPG interventionist strategy was so broadly defined as to include every region of the world and a vast array of political, economic, and military situations that could trigger the deployment of U.S. armed forces. The White House should not flinch from a willingness to dictate global, regional, and internal power configurations and promote "open economic systems" which benefit U.S. interests:

> While the U.S. cannot become the world's "policeman," by assuming responsibility for righting every wrong, we will retain the preeminent responsibility for addressing selectively those wrongs which threaten not only our interests, but those of our allies or friends, or which could seriously unsettle international relations. Various types of U.S. interests may be involved in such instances: access to vital raw materials, primarily Persian Gulf oil; proliferation of weapons of mass destruction and ballistic missiles; threats to U.S. citizens from terrorism or regional or local conflict; and threats to U.S. society from narcotics trafficking.[22]

Retaining military supremacy and preparing for direct intervention were also tied to a strategy of deterring or intimidating rivals among the advanced capitalist countries from developing their own military capacities to challenge U.S. global pretensions:

> Our first objective is to prevent the reemergence of a new rival, either on the territory of the former Soviet Union or elsewhere, that poses a threat on the order of that posed formerly by the Soviet Union. This . . . requires that we endeavor to prevent any hostile power from dominating a region whose resources would, under consoli-

> dated control, be sufficient to generate global power. These regions include Western Europe, East Asia, the territory of the former Soviet Union, and Southwest Asia. . . . Finally, we must maintain the mechanisms for deterring potential competitors from ever aspiring to a larger regional or global role. [23]

Relying on its military supremacy, the U.S. seeks to intimidate Japan and Germany, and preempt any military buildups commensurate with their economic power and growing political influence. Dominating and threatening, Washington ultimately hopes to regain privileged access to markets and resources, and retain influence in key regions of strategic importance where its economic power is waning.

Washington's pursuit of global power focuses on a variety of policy instrumentalities depending on the U.S. capacity to manipulate them for its use. At no point did the DPG document refer to the United States acting exclusively through any collective body such as the United Nations—a recognition that other countries may not share the White House's policies and interests in global dominance. Thus, Washington develops a "flexible" approach, using collective bodies and citing international law when it suits its global design and discarding them for unilateral military intervention or coalitions of allies and clients when it decides to act in opposition to those organizations. The DPG noted that "coalitions" hold considerable promise for promoting "collective action" as in the Persian Gulf War but that "we should expect future coalitions to be ad hoc assemblies often not lasting beyond the crisis being confronted, and in many cases carrying only general agreement over the objectives to be accomplished." What is most important, it says, is "the sense that the world order is ultimately backed by the U.S." and "the United States should be postured to act independently when collective action cannot be orchestrated" or in a crisis demanding a rapid response. [24] The White House decisions to invade Grenada (1983) and Panama (1989), for instance, were taken without reference to either the United Nations or the Organization of American States— in the knowledge that prevailing sentiment in these bodies opposed both projections of U.S. military power.

In Europe, the Bush White House repeatedly emphasized the need to maintain a pivotal role for NATO in the post-Cold War era—an organization in which American power and influence has always predominated. Not surprisingly, it was extremely critical of French-German bilateral security proposals leading to the possible establishment of a continental military force. One such initiative, a joint 35,000-man army corp, was interpreted by Washington as an attempt to undermine U.S. leadership of the Western military alliance.[25] The DPG was quite explicit regarding the need to avoid the development of any European security organization that could supplant NATO, thereby profoundly diminishing America's authority over the continent:

> NATO continues to provide the indispensable foundation for a stable security environment in Europe. Therefore, it is of fundamental importance to preserve NATO as the primary instrument of Western defense and security, as well as the channel for U.S. influence and participation in European security affairs. While the United States supports the goal of European integration, we must seek to prevent the emergence of European-only security arrangements which would undermine NATO, particularly the alliance's integrated command structure.[26]

Not only is Washington determined to keep NATO's presence as a mechanism for sustaining U.S. influence in Europe, it also seeks to extend its hegemony east to the former Warsaw Pact nations. By developing military linkages and "security commitments," it could reestablish direct military ties with regimes in Central and Eastern Europe and thereby counteract the growing German and West European influence in regional politics. Also, once security commitments are in place, Washington could have a basis for intervening if the decaying free-market regimes are challenged by renewed leftist-oriented political movements, as it has done in Asia and Latin America.

Confronting the new realities of inter-capitalist rivalries, the DPG addressed the importance of undermining the German and Japanese challenges to U.S. global and even regional power. This fundamental strategic objective reflected the unabashedly imperial nature of

Washington's drive for undisputed world supremacy: "There are other potential nations or coalitions that could, in the further future, develop strategic aims and a defense posture of region-wide or global domination. Our strategy must now refocus on precluding the emergence of any potential future global competitor."[27]

While assuming an aggressive posture toward advanced capitalist rivals, the DPG also stressed the need to extend U.S. influence over the new republics of the former Soviet Union through establishing political ties ("a democratic partnership") and economic linkages (supporting efforts to shift to "market-based economies"), all the time promoting asymmetrical disarmament, with the ultimate aim of consolidating advantageous patron-client relations—at the expense of its would-be imperial rivals. The document suggested a greater involvement of "the east-central Europeans" in Western political, economic, and military organizations, including "an expanded NATO liaison. . . . The U.S. could also consider extending to the east-central European states security commitments analogous to those we have extended to Persian Gulf states."[28]

And just as it was imperative to undermine German influence in Europe, through NATO and unilaterally, it was equally necessary to project sufficient force in the Asia-Pacific region to counteract the threat of "a regional hegemon" emerging in that part of the world. This none-too-subtle allusion to Japan reflected a concern that went beyond its economic dominance in this area—its ability to outcompete and displace American products from Asian markets—to include the "potentially destabilizing" consequences that might flow from any increase in Tokyo's existing military capabilities. All the more reason to move quickly and aggressively to undercut its influence:

> To buttress the vital political and economic relationships we have along the Pacific rim, we must maintain our status as a military power of the first magnitude in the area. This will enable the U.S. to continue to contribute to regional security and stability by acting as a balancing force and prevent emergence of a vacuum or a regional hegemon . . . we must also remain sensitive to the potentially destabilizing effects that enhanced roles on the part of our allies, particularly Japan but also possibly Korea might produce.[29]

The best way of minimizing the "potentially destabilizing effects" of a unified Korea, according to the DPG, was to avoid any rupture in bilateral ties: "[The U.S.] should seek to maintain an alliance relationship with a unified democratic Korea."[30]

The pattern of forming military alliances with client regimes to retain U.S. regional influence and power extended to the Middle East and Southwest Africa where "our overall objective is to remain the predominant outside power in the region and reserve U.S. and Western access to the region's oil. We also seek to . . . protect U.S. nationals and property. . . . As demonstrated by Iraq's invasion of Kuwait, it remains fundamentally important to prevent a hegemon or alignment of powers from dominating the region." Clearly, in the world of the defense planners, democracy and self-determination in the Third World takes second place to the imperial state's access to strategic raw materials, its protection of "U.S. nationals and property" and its intention "to remain the predominant outside power" in the Middle East and elsewhere.[31]

Where countries have successfully resisted U.S. global and regional domination, Washington looks to create external provocation or to exploit domestic dissent to impose what it calls positive changes—a euphemism for regimes favorably disposed to U.S. global aspirations. The example of Cuba is illustrative:

> Cuba's growing domestic crisis holds out the prospect for positive change, but over the near term, Cuba's tenuous internal situation is likely to generate new challenges to U.S. policy. Consequently, our programs must provide capabilities to meet a variety of Cuban contingencies which could include an attempted repetition of the Mariel boatlift, a military provocation against the U.S. or an American ally, or political instability and internal conflict in Cuba.[32]

President Bush affirmed his broad support for the DPG advocacy of U.S. global supremacy, declaring that whether Washington assumed the burden of world policing alone or worked through multilateral organizations, "we are leaders and must continue to lead."[33] However, the dominant theme of subordinating Germany and Japan to U.S. hegemonic ambitions was so bluntly stated as to create disquiet among some White House and State Department officials.[34]

This concern was reflected in a revised (April 1992) version of the document which eliminated or toned down the unilateral language of the earlier draft but without fundamentally altering its basic thrust. While Japan and Germany were no longer described as potential "regional hegemons" and hostile references to allied efforts to set up European-only security arrangements were expunged, much of what was explicit in the original document simply became implicit in the new one.

Essentially, the revisions were cosmetic in nature, shaped by domestic political concerns and the need to assuage the concerns and sensibilities of NATO governments. For example, instead of talking about the "potentially destabilizing" affects for Asia of rising Japanese and Korean military power, the two nations were now advised to move "prudently" in building up "their defensive capabilities." Whereas the February draft spoke of "preventing Russia . . . from reestablishing a hegemonic position in Eastern Europe" through NATO or unilateral U.S. military action, the toned-down language of the April document referred to the importance of establishing a "zone of peace" in Central and Eastern Europe and called for a new consensus within NATO (whose traditional historic role had to be preserved) on the "important security interests . . . at stake for both the Europeans and for us in Central and Eastern Europe."[35] A senior administration official observed that the Pentagon would not be unduly concerned about these changes: the "clear message" remains but "without raising some of the same froth" of the earlier draft.[36]

While the April document expressed a "preference" for acting in concert and cooperation with allies when confronted by global or regional "threats," it nonetheless reemphasized the U.S. determination to act unilaterally "as necessary, to protect our critical interests" or to prevent "any hostile power from dominating a region critical to our interests." Collective military responses are not ruled out but they are seen as dependent on American initiative and leadership: "Only a nation that is strong enough to act decisively can provide the leadership that is needed to encourage others to resist aggression. . . . [Collective security] worked in the [Persian Gulf] because the

United States was willing and able to provide . . . leadership." At the same time, international bodies cannot be allowed to obstruct the United States in the pursuit of its policy objectives: "While the United States cannot become the world's policeman . . . neither can we allow our critical interests to depend solely on international mechanisms that can be blocked by countries whose interests may be very different from our own."[37]

CONCLUSION

The Bush White House was intent on recreating a world of uncontested U.S. power, in the process subordinating the ambitions of competitor allies to American interests, defining their roles on a global scale and within regional spheres. Treating allies like banana republics sharply contradicted the public rhetoric committing Washington to take account of their interests and involve them in alliance decision making. In large part, this "politics of domination and subordination" strategy was built around the retention of massive military superiority over its capitalist competitors, a willingness to project that power in regions of contention, unilaterally or with ad hoc coalitions, and a deepening of alliances with internationally oriented capitalist sectors—especially in the countries of the Third World.

During his valedictory foreign policy address in December 1992, George Bush emphatically reaffirmed this priority of striving for world hegemony. Echoing the academic imperial revivalists, he declared that American "leadership" and "power" were prerequisites for a stable international order; that "American leadership [means] economic, political and, yes, military"; that, in all three respects, it embodied "a hard-nosed sense of American self-interest." Dismissing those who "assert that domestic needs preclude an active foreign policy," he pontificated that "the alternative to American leadership is not more security for our citizens but less; not the flourishing of American principles but their isolation in a world actively held hostile to them."[38]

The strategy and the case for U.S. world domination raises several questions: To what extent does it reflect wishful thinking, projections into the future, or simply rationales for maintaining military budgets? If it does represent serious strategic thinking, to what extent does the U.S. have the capacity to realize those goals? There is no mention in either the DPG or the Bush speech of the economic forces that can complement military power, no discussion of the economic decay of the domestic foundations to sustain a global police role, interventions, and the like. It is simply presumed that the national economy can sustain this "reach" for undisputed world supremacy. If global power does have an adverse impact on the U.S. domestic economy, what are the political costs—does there exist a political basis or will to extend global power with a deteriorating domestic economy?

There are further questions concerning the reactions of U.S. "allies" as imperial rivals. To what extent will they allow Washington to use its policy instruments to intimidate and subordinate them to U.S. global designs? How does the United States use its military superiority to achieve economic power and regain lost control in regions already under adversarial influence? French officials have attacked what they perceive to be America's increasing arrogance in the post-bipolar world, reflected in a pronounced tendency to bypass European allies, or take their support for granted, in devising policies toward the Middle East and Eastern Europe in particular.[39] During 1992 talks between French Foreign Minister Roland Dumas and U.S. Secretary of State James Baker about outstanding economic, security, and political differences, the discussion became so acrimonious that Baker at one point challenged his French opposite number: "Are you for us or against us?"[40] Likewise, Germany's economic power within Europe and Japan's influence in Asia has served as the basis for a more independent diplomacy while simultaneously generating numerous economic conflicts with Washington. Germany and Japan's political and strategic dependence on the United States—the goal of postwar imperial state policy—has long since passed.[41]

With the return to center stage of Big Power rivalries, traditional imperial politics has reasserted itself in the post-Cold War era.

Growing inter-capitalist competition, and Washington's efforts to subordinate senior alliance partners to its global leadership, poses a major challenge to those many analysts who believed that the end of the Cold War would bring about an era of peace and prosperity. As the 1992 Defense Planning Guidance document suggests, U.S. expansion and hegemonic aspirations were not a response to the Cold War or the Soviet "threat," but a product of politico-economic institutions in American society. This study emphasizes the fundamentally negative impact the U.S. vision will have, or is already having, on world peace and national economies. First, it prefigures more Big Power interventions to shape political and economic outcomes, particularly in countries seeking to assert their independence from Washington. Second, rising conflict and competition among these capitalist bloc rivals is likely to accelerate the diversion of resources from domestic economies to sustain outward-looking elites—with the consequent fall in living standards at home. However, we contend that, even on its own terms, U.S. global policy is unworkable because of domestic constraints and the changes that have taken place in the international arena. Such unstable foundations cannot sustain this drive for world dominance.

This study does not merely argue that assertions of unilateral power are dangerous and unworkable; nor does it advocate replacing unilateral politics with some kind of alliance "power sharing" arrangement. Rather, it questions the very premises of imperial policy which maintain that it can lead to a New World Order of peace, prosperity, and equity. The issue is not unilateralism versus multilateralism, whether the United States should be the world's sole policeman or share duties with Europe and Japan. Both are variants of the new imperial policies that have emerged in the post-Cold War era.

The New World Order that Washington has attempted to fashion entering the 1990s, based partly on the notion of subordinating Europe and Japan to U.S. global ends, bears little or no relation to contemporary international reality. On the contrary, it speaks to a degree of voluntarism born of a blighted vision—one that looks only at the ideological and military role of power, not the economic; one that looks only at U.S.-Third World military and ideological gains and ignores U.S. failures in market competition; one that looks backward to a past era of U.S. dominance and averts its gaze at the present and future world of relatively equal competitors; one that celebrates ideological victories over communism, military victories over "terrorist states" (Iraq) and the overthrow of Third World nationalist governments (often at the cost of enormous human devastation), and ignores the hollowing out of urban capitalism in America. The blind spots are not minor; they are major determinants of global power and strategic failures.

In the following chapters we argue that the U.S. military and ideological hegemony is not matched by economic capacity; that while global American economic actors are expanding and securing markets, they do so with the support of an imperial state presiding over a decaying urban economy, a disaffected public, and an increasingly disreputable political system. The drive for world leadership in political, military, and ideological spheres is directly related to the national socioeconomic spheres.

2

THE DECLINE OF U.S. ECONOMIC POWER AT HOME AND ABROAD

Basic changes in the structure of U.S. capitalism have been under way during the past twenty years. Several studies have pointed to the declining role of industrial capital, which no longer is the foundation upon which the economy stands.[1] One school of analysis has detected the emergence of a postindustrial, high-technology information economy, while another has emphasized the ascendancy of finance, real estate, and speculative capital.[2] For writers who have argued the latter—where a high-risk, high-expected-return mentality predominates—the growth of the "junk bond" market has been a potent symbol. The total number of junk bonds outstanding rose from about 1 million in 1977 to over 45 million in 1986.[3] The growth of this paper economy created an increasingly volatile climate punctuated by wild fluctuations of the stock market and burgeoning corporate indebtedness.

An examination of data on the major industrial sources of wealth of the 400 richest Americans, the so-called "Forbes 400," for the period 1982 to 1988 offers revealing evidence of the extent to which the wealth of the nation's richest capitalists has decisively shifted away from industry and toward such speculative forms as finance and real estate.[4]

A strikingly large percentage of the Forbes 400, 38%, had the major sources of their wealth in finance and real estate in 1988, followed at a distance by manufacturing (19%) and the mass media (18%). Equally impressive is the growth during the 1980s of the dominance of the "paper economy" (finance and real estate) over manufacturing. In 1983, only 25% of the very wealthy had their assets in the paper economy, about the same as in manufacturing. Between 1983 and 1988, the percentage whose wealth was concentrated in the paper economy increased by half, while the percentage concentrated in manufacturing declined noticeably. The route to the top of the economy has clearly shifted from productive to unproductive effort and, by implication, to speculative endeavor. There is scant evidence to justify the claim that the United States has shifted from being an industrial society to being an information society. The proportion of top capitalists with their main wealth in the high-tech sector, which was only 3% in 1983, was no more than 4% in 1988. The spread between the paper economy and high-tech actually widened from twenty-two percentage points in 1983 to thirty-four percentage points in 1988. Clearly, the very wealthy who have their money in high-tech operate in a milieu dominated by more numerous and powerful colleagues in the paper economy.

The declining importance of "sun belt" capitalists—the oil and gas crowd—is also striking. In 1983, they made up 16% of the very wealthy, but by 1988 only 8%. The collapse of oil prices, the over-indebtedness of the speculative petroleum sector, and increased takeover activity played a major role in thinning the ranks of the oil barons.

Further confirmation of the ascendancy of finance and real estate capital is evident in the growing revenue accruing to security brokers and dealers during the 1980s; the number of companies engaged in the speculative sector (brokerage houses) and in the growth of bank holding companies. Between 1983 and 1989, revenues to security brokers and dealers increased four and a half times, the number of brokerage firms more than doubled, while bank holdings rose almost fourfold.[5]

The rising power of these forms of unproductive capital and the relative decline of industrial capital in the last decade coincided with growing concentration and centralization of capital—the so-called merger madness. Although the intensification of merger activity had been going on for some time, it took a dramatic new form in the hands of speculator capitalists. Buyouts were no longer long-term investments, sites for new production, diversification, and innovation, or even means to capture control over competitors' markets. The emphasis was now on maximizing short-term returns by stripping and selling off valuable assets and/or reselling the enterprises for a quick turnover profit.[6] An important mechanism in the speculative turnover of ownership during the 1980s was the leveraged buyout (LBO), whose volume jumped from $1 billion in 1980 to $59 billion in 1988. But LBOs were only part of the picture; non-LBOs increased from $30 billion to $257 billion in the same period.

The buyout environment had a significant impact on managerial strategy, which was increasingly directed toward short-run gains to satisfy stockholders. Managers argued that "investors are short-sighted, compelling management to sacrifice long-term investment and maximize current earnings—or else face the threat of takeover."[7] As one author put it:

> . . . there is intense pressure for current earnings. So the message is: Don't get caught with long-term investments. And leverage the hell out of yourself. Do all the things we used to consider bad management.[8]

"ERODING THE FOUNDATIONS":
THE IMPACT OF FINANCIAL CAPITAL

The commanding presence of finance capital in the American economy since the early 1980s, inextricably linked to the decline of the United States as a global economic power, was in large part made possible by the deregulation of the banking system which facilitated a massive shift of capital away from productive, goods-producing activities. Industrial investments were subordinated to the funding of military and speculator regimes abroad (Latin America) and to a preoccupation with junk bonds, LBOs, and commercial real estate at home. Banks not only tripled their real estate lending during the decade but also provided between 50% and 70% of the capital for the purchase of LBOs. By the end of 1988, total bank loans to LBOs were estimated at $175 billion to $200 billion.[9]

Whether at home or abroad, the very short-term "strength" of finance capital in displacing productivity undermined the substantive activities that supported the paper exchanges.

Deregulation of financial activity stimulated the drive for short-term, risk-free profits since bankers and financiers were free to run up losses without any obligation to pay the costs in the knowledge that the Federal Deposit Insurance Corporation (FDIC) would ultimately assume responsibility if and when the risks led to bankruptcy. Injudicious lending to the Third World and the incapacity of corporate takeover artists and real estate developers to repay multimillion dollar loans triggered the collapse of over 1,000 banks between 1985 and 1992, the near failure of hundreds more, and left an additional 1,500 financial institutions so undercapitalised as to be technically insolvent. Over the same period, banks' nonperforming real estate assets more than doubled to $90.5 billion; so did write-offs that totalled almost $10 billion in 1992.[10] By the end of 1990, bank losses had already virtually exhausted the FDIC insurance fund: its holdings plummeted to $8.4 billion or less than 40 cents for every $100 of insured deposits in the United States, more than three times below the $1.25 that regulators defined as a safe level.[11]

These bank failures, including the massive savings and loan debacle which could eventually cost the government up to $500 billion in bailout payments, cannot be attributed simply to an easing of federal controls or inadequate safeguards. They were symptomatic of a larger political context in which financial capital established undisputed hegemony over public institutions, thus turning "regulators" into instruments or tacit accomplices of the bankers' objectives. Both Democratic and Republican Parties, as well as Congress and the executive, played active roles in promoting and encouraging the expansion of finance capital while assorted academics and media pundits tendered their support, proclaiming the advent of a crisis-free, postindustrial information society. The latter conveniently neglected to mention that the technology and information was largely wired by banking houses to promote financial speculation. While adopting "free-market rhetoric," the "entrepreneurs" were speculating with public money, since the government was the backstop, insuring all deposits. Statism in the service of dollar speculation defined the "populism" of the bankers. "Free market" became the formula for fleecing depositors, dismantling industry, and saddling the government with the obligation to "socialize" the losses. Such behavior, however, testified to the considerable influence this financial class wielded in the national political arena.

To blame the "regulators" or the "rules" is to reduce a global political problem to a technical/administrative one—a view reinforced upon consideration of the tenuous position of the major commercial banks, supposedly the conservative leaders in the corporate financial sector. If criminal "fraud" was the pervasive accompaniment of the free-market policies that led the savings and loan industry on the road to bankruptcy, then honest speculation was the path to the disasters that befell some of the country's most prominent commercial banks. These financial institutions were willing to finance the pillage of American industry in part through their laundering of drug monies while forcefully and successfully resisting efforts at regulation. Bank officials argued that congressional legislation denying the use of Federal Reserve wire transfer facilities and New York Clearing Houses Inter-Bank Payments systems to any bank that failed to honor a subpoena for records in connection with a drug investigation would drive narco dollars to overseas banks and weaken the dollar currency.[12] Honest speculation and sordid drug laundering kept the U.S. balance of payments deficit from growing by keeping money at home that subsequently hollowed out the nation's industrial sector.

The very success of finance capital, the scope and depth of its activity in devouring competition and displacing alternative sources for investment, contained the seeds of its demise. Speculation on a narrow real economy ultimately overvalued its own nonproductive resources and undermined the value-producing economic activities upon which the speculative bubble fundamentally rested. The financial "revolution" ended up consuming its principal architects. The prototypical case has been Citicorp, the largest American bank in terms of assets ($224 billion) and overseas offices (in around ninety countries).

Citicorp's spiralling loan losses, rising from $1.9 billion in 1989 to $2.9 billion in 1990 to $5 billion in 1991, were the outcome of three periods of speculative activity: loans totalling almost $15 billion to "free-market" Third World military and civilian regimes during the 1970s and 1980s that turned sour costing the bank $4 billion; a shift to financing commercial real estate during the latter half of the 1980s that culminated in losses exceeding $600 million during 1990–91; and a third period of speculative activity that saw the bank plunge into the financing of corporate takeovers only to experience such unmitigated disasters as its involvement with the Canadian speculator, and subsequently bankrupt, Robert Campeau. He borrowed hundreds of millions of dollars from Citicorp in failed efforts to gain control of several up-market American department store chains. The end result of the second and third speculative "waves" was catastrophic: in September 1991, Citicorp reported that 24.4% of its loans for commercial real estate were "badly troubled" while the FDIC used identical language in reference to 25.8% of loans by the country's largest bank to highly indebted companies. Between 1986 and 1991, Citicorp's nonperforming assets tripled from $3 billion to more than $10 billion. Its vulnerability, however, is even more clearly seen in the ratio of loan losses (over $9 billion) to reserves (less than $6 billion).[13]

The precarious financial status of Citicorp was replicated throughout the U.S. commercial banking fraternity. As America entered the 1990s, losses exceeded reserves in seven of the other ten largest banks in the nation: Bank of America, Chase Manhattan, Security Pacific, Chemical Banking, NCNB, Manufacturers Hanover, and First Interstate. In September 1990, Chase Manhattan announced it would cut costs by $300 million annually and that it expected a third-quarter loss of $625 million.[14] The ratios of capital to assets for eight of the ten largest banks were under 5% (and for four out of ten under 3%), raising the specter that a series of defaults could bring the institutions down—with a large ripple effect throughout the financial system. Meanwhile, in the nation as a whole, over a thousand banks holding 12.1% ($408.8 billion) of all banking assets, up from 7.1% in 1989, were deemed "vulnerable to failure."[15]

As U.S. banks moved toward high-profit, high-risk speculative ventures in the form of junk bonds, LBOs, commercial real estate, and overseas loans to free-market speculator regimes, their global position sharply declined while domestic competition from foreign banks increased. Between 1960 and 1990, the combined percentage of total assets of the world's twelve largest banks that were Japanese, German, and French owned increased from 0% to 94%; the percentage held by U.S. banks declined from 61% to 0%.[16] Twenty years ago, six of the world's top twenty banks (by assets) were American-owned; in 1990, only two U.S. banks were ranked in the top fifty (Citicorp at 22nd; Bank of America at 49th). At the same time, 41 cents of every dollar held by the world's 100 largest banks were in Japanese financial institutions compared with only 11 cents in U.S.-owned banks.[17] Between 1984 and 1988, the number of large U.S. banking companies monitored by the Federal Reserve Board with overseas branches declined from 163 to 132 and the number of branches from 917 to 849. The decline in the foreign assets of U.S. banks was even more dramatic: from $343 billion in 1981 to $275 billion in 1988.[18]

Inside the United States, the 1980s witnessed a significant rise in foreign bank loans which were growing at a rate almost three times that of domestic banks toward the end of the decade. Japanese banks accounted for over 10% of U.S. bank assets nationwide, controlled five of the ten largest banks in California, and had emerged as major actors (controlling close to 25%) in the commercial loan market.[19] The share of Japanese financial assets deposited in U.S. banks also jumped dramatically, from 11.5% in 1984 to 32.1% in 1988.[20]

Unquestionably, the era of the ascendancy of finance capital profoundly eroded the domestic foundations and overseas position of U.S. industrial capital. At home, the financing of LBOs absorbed huge amounts of potential investment capital, led to large-scale indebtedness, and often bankruptcy, of firms; the division of capital toward LBOs, as well as junk bonds and real estate speculation, undermined any industrial policy oriented toward large-scale, long-term investments in research and development. The very "growth" of the financial sector occurred precisely at the expense of industrial capital, through the pillage and weakening of the industrial-techno-logical sector—thus ensuring its declining ability to compete globally.

While U.S. banks vastly improved their overall balance sheets during the veritable "explosion" of high-interest lending to the Third World, particularly Latin America in the 1970s, the medium and long-term consequences for U.S. manufacturers were disastrous. The rising debt payments burden contracted regional export markets by over one-third during the following decade. Hence, the paradox that mainland industries now lacked lucrative markets in an area of undisputed U.S. hegemony. Subsequent debt-swap arrangements, the dismantling of tariff barriers and foreign investment controls, and the denationalization of public enterprises opened short-term profitable opportunities for American bankers and multinationals, but gains of this kind in a stagnant and shrinking market are incapable of fuelling world power pretensions.

Finance capital eroded the industrial cushion from which recovery would have emerged; it undermined the government's capacity to stimulate the domestic economy through public spending by loading down federal budgets with huge private sector bailouts. At the same time, finance capital in speculator mode eroded its own position by undermining Third World trading partners with its one-sided pursuit of free market policies, thus extending deindustrialization from the U.S. heartland to the global periphery.

The post-1980 hegemonic position of this form of capital in the United States, and the speculative environment it encouraged, defined the context and meaning of the technological innovations and the content of the "information" revolution. High-tech computer systems were geared toward absorbing and processing a wealth of information about speculative activity and thus worked against the productive context from which they came. Such systems facilitated massive transfers of funds from one industry to another, mobilizing resources for LBOs that ultimately undermined the application of technology to the production of saleable and competitive goods in the world marketplace.

The contrast with its major capitalist competitors, who have equally highly developed and powerful financial systems, is striking. Whereas in the United States finance capital was delinked from an expanding industrial system in favor of growing ties with real estate developers unable to fend off bankruptcy and stagnant Third World regimes, and was unable to enlist the support of an equally overindebted government to stimulate recovery, in Germany and Japan the situation was just the opposite. There, the links between finance capital and industry, mediated by activist states, provided the wherewithal for large-scale financing for new products and the application of new technological innovations, thus increasing global competitiveness.

Instead of a financial system increasingly tied to high-risk, high-return speculative activities in the nonproductive service sector, the German and Japanese states harnessed finance capital to the construction of a dynamic and expanding industrial capital able to compete in the global marketplace. During the 1980s, for example, they held down interest rates on loans for capital goods (equipment and machinery) purchases to approximately two-thirds the U.S. level.[21]

The Japanese state has played an influential role in getting its banks to fund targeted government industries such as computers, electronics, robotics, and biotechnology on attractive terms in return for which it has effectively guaranteed them (through the Central Bank) against losses.[22] The experience of the NEC Corporation, one of the world's largest makers of computer chips, is illustrative. When NEC decided to invest hundreds of millions of dollars in semiconductor plants in the late 1970s, major banks provided more than one-third of the loans and made commitments to fund the company's growth on a long-term basis. "We don't have to worry about a shortage of funds to finance a long-term strategy," explained NEC executive Susumu Kitazawa, "Even if we get into difficulty, we know our main bank will provide assistance without fail."[23]

In Germany, the interlocking and reciprocal ties between the country's major industrial corporations and finance capital may be even more prominent. While many top corporations own shares in major banks and their executives sit on the supervisory boards of these institutions, bankers sit on the boards of almost every major German industrial corporation. In fact, the ten largest banks hold majority control in twenty-seven of the thirty-two biggest industrial firms and, according to some estimates, have a substantial stake in nearly every one of the top fifty companies.[24]

As Tokyo and Bonn flexed their economic muscle on a world scale, the question that loomed for Washington at the beginning of the 1990s was not whether the U.S. economy could recover its global leadership, but whether there were sufficient economic resources to prevent a major financial collapse. And while bank losses and insolvency rates hit record levels not approached since the Great Depression, the depositors' "safety net," the FDIC, was constantly running out of funds and was dependent on an increasingly reluctant Congress to authorize new bailout packages to supplement its dwindling resources.[25]

UNCOMPETITIVE ABROAD: THE NATIONAL ECONOMY IN RELATIVE DECLINE

The U.S. economy has been on a downward curve for at least a decade. The evidence is overwhelming. The indicators of decline are both general and specific. The role of finance capital in shaping this larger universe has been pivotal. Corporate raiders and leveraged buyout speculators received greater incentives for borrowing than saving, interest payments were exempted from taxes, investment funds were diverted from productive activities (R&D, capital goods, and plants) into mergers and buyouts. While companies spent billions on mergers and acquisitions, and corporate debt tripled to $2.2 trillion during the 1980s, the 2% of national income going into new net business investment annually represented a drop of over 40% compared with the 1960-80 period.[26] In 1988 alone, the United States incurred nearly $120 billion in foreign debt to attain a level of plant and equipment investment per worker that was still only half the Japanese rate. Observing these developments, the chairman of Sony Corporation Akio Morita made a telling comment: "Americans make money by playing 'money game,' namely, mergers and acquisitions, by simply moving money back and forth . . . instead of creating and producing goods with some actual value."[27]

America's dependence on overseas borrowings to finance a $4 trillion-plus federal debt, growing at almost $1 billion daily, increased at an unprecedented rate during the Reagan/Bush era. Japanese financiers, attracted by high real interest rates, invested an estimated $90 billion in U.S. Treasury securities. By the late 1980s, foreign claims on U.S. assets reached $1.5 trillion (including government bonds, stocks, etc.), almost equivalent to the total value of all the companies listed on Wall Street's stock exchange. Debt interest payments quadrupled in just over a decade. Toward the end of this speculative era, annual debt servicing absorbed an extraordinary 40% of all federal individual income tax revenues ($200 billion).[28] Between 1982 and 1990, the United States borrowed almost $700 billion more than it lent in a failing effort to accumulate sufficient funds for domestic investment in a context of rising budget deficits (quadrupled in the 1980s to $320 billion, and has continued its upward spiral since, breaking the $350 billion mark in 1992) and falling savings rates.[29] The U.S. foreign debt was four times greater than the German debt and almost fifty times what Japan owes to its global creditors; it amounted to $1,572 for every American citizen compared to a minuscule $75 that every Japanese "owed" abroad.[30]

If the major beneficiaries of this process were foreign and domestic finance capital, the big loser has been the contracting American industrial economy. On the one hand, the impact of the debt interest burden on public investment spending in the 1980s was catastrophic; the funding of road, highway, education, training, and other programs declined by 30%.[31] On the other hand, in its effort to finance the skyrocketing debt, the federal government made the bidding for loans in the marketplace more competitive; this, in turn, forced up interest rates and thus "crowded out" productive capital which found it increasingly difficult to pay the added costs of borrowing.

For the first time this century, interest payments on past debts exceed new investments. And even statistics, disastrous as they are, may understate the extent of the problem in the light of periodic dubious White House transfers and bookkeeping procedures. In 1990, for example, the *New York Times* reported that the Bush administration had shifted over $450 billion in Social Security funds to help cover the deficit and also decided to classify as "off budget" the multibillion savings and loan bailout packages.[32]

The U.S. merchandise trade deficit with the rest of the world ranged between $100 billion and $200 billion through much of the 1980s, dominated by an average annual imbalance with Japan of around $40 billion. Although the global deficit fell from $159 billion in 1987 to $66 billion in 1991, it surged back to $84.3 billion in 1992 (a 29% increase), reflecting the fact that the growth in exports was still not keeping pace with imports. Moreover, this upward trend can be expected to continue, largely due to the persistent strong demand for Japanese imports—that produced a 14% increase (to $43.7 billion) in that country's trade surplus with the U.S. in 1992. Furthermore, while the trade deficit with Japan fell by $16 billion between 1987 and 1991, the decline was more illusory than real because it was accompanied by a substantial increase in U.S. purchases of goods produced by Japanese-owned manufacturing plants located in Southeast Asia.[33] Clearly, Japan's trade expansion is centered on its "productive" export side, America's on its "compradore" import side. Deficits also began to show up in the services and investment sector of the American economy where international surpluses have long been relied on to offset deficits in merchandise trade—further evidence suggesting a declining U.S. capacity to compete in world markets and a future increasingly mortgaged to overseas capitalists.

Numerous specific indicators also highlight the process of domestic decline: between 1979 and 1991, U.S. factories lost domestic market share in all twenty-six basic industries—from machine tools to computers to automobiles.[34] In the latter sector, Detroit's "Big Three" manufacturers not only lost market share but also became increasingly dependent on their Japanese competitors amid announcements by General Motors of plant closings and tens of thousands of worker layoffs. In 1984, the "Big Three" controlled 76.1%

of the American market while Japan and other foreign producers accounted for 23.9%; by 1991, Japanese carmakers alone had captured over 30% of the market. But if automobiles fully produced in Japan and sold to General Motors and Chrysler (over 164,000 in 1991), or at Japanese or joint-venture "transplants" in the United States, are included, the real figure exceeded 36%. In fact, some estimates place Tokyo's share of U.S. retail auto sales—excluding Detroit's sales to the car rental businesses—at close to 50%. And, in the absence of U.S. government-imposed quota restrictions on Japanese exports, the rate of decline in Detroit's market share would have been substantially greater.[35]

In the areas of industrial and high-technology development, the U.S. seriously lags behind its major competitors. Its global competitive position in an array of critical industrial sectors began to markedly decline in the 1960s and 1970s, reaching a nadir in the late 1980s. Between 1960 and 1980, based on the percentages of consolidated sales of the world's twelve largest companies in each industry, the U.S. global market share contracted from 83% to 42% in automobiles, 71% to 44% in electrical equipment and electronics, 74% to 26% in iron and steel, 63% to 21% in nonferrous metals, 87% to 55% in pharmaceuticals, and 68% to 31% in chemicals. During this same period, the combined Japan-Germany share of automobiles increased from 7% to 31% while that of iron and steel rose from 16% to 55%; Japan's share of electrical equipment and electronics sales went from 8% to 21%; and Germany's share of chemical sales doubled from 18% to 36%. One of the few exceptions to this trend was in aerospace where the U.S. maintained its dominant position, experiencing only an incremental decline in world market share from 85% in 1960 to 81% in 1980.

Between 1980 and 1990, the pace of eroding U.S. industrial competitiveness quickened. Its world market share (based on the twelve largest companies) declined fourfold to 11% for electrical equipment and electronics, slumped from 21% to 16% for nonferrous metals, from 31% to 23% for chemicals sales. Meanwhile, Germany and Japan continued to surge. The latter's worldwide sales of nonferrous metals climbed from 18% to 44% while Bonn's performance in the electrical equipment/electronics sector (from 21% to 47%) was equally impressive. In the areas of chemicals, Germany's global market share rose 3% in contrast to an 8% decline in America's share. In the battle for world automobile supremacy, the combined Germany-Japan sales (from 31% to 44%) surpassed Detroit's "Big Three" (from 42% to 38%) for the first time. Only in aerospace among the key sectors did the U.S. buck this trend (79% of world market share in 1990); although even this globally competitive sector was not safe from foreign takeovers. Witness Taiwan Bero Space's acquisition of 40% of McDonnell Douglas' commercial sector and a Japanese consortium's 20% purchase of Boeing Corporation.

The disappearance of U.S. firms from the lists of the world's top twelve over the past three decades attests to this declining industrial competitiveness. In 1960, for example, the United States had six electrical equipment/electronics firms, seven iron and steel companies, eight nonferrous enterprises, and eight chemical corporations in the top twelve of each of these categories; by 1990, the figures were one (1988), zero, two, and three respectively.[36] In 1970, sixty-four of the world's largest industrial corporations were in the United States and only thirty-four in Europe and Japan. Almost two decades later (1988), the U.S. total had dropped to forty-two while the Europe/Japan number had risen to forty-eight.[37]

Other examples of declining U.S. competitiveness include such key areas as critical technologies and machine tools. Japan's global market share of the semiconductor (computer chips) industry increased from 37.4% in 1981 to 51% in 1988 while the U.S. share plummeted from 48.9% to around 35%.[38] For the first time, U.S. combat troops (during the 1990 Persian Gulf hostilities) became dependent on overseas suppliers (especially Japan and France) for chips, transistors, and other electronic parts for their advanced weapons.[39] U.S. losses to Japan in this area extended to the sophisticated machinery used to make computer chips. American companies' market share of wafer fabrication equipment, which etches circuits into silicon, fell from 62% in 1982 to 45% in 1987 while the share accruing to Japanese companies rose from 29% to 44%. Through the 1980s, the United States also lost out to the Japanese in the production of ceramic packages used to house computer chips.[40] Regarding machine tools, often called "the semiconductors of the manufacturing world," the number of domestic manufacturers fell from 1,400 in 1982 to 600 in 1987. Not surprisingly, the United States dropped from first to fourth in production behind Japan, West Germany, and the Soviet Union. In 1991, the United States accounted for only 10% of the world's machine tool market.[41]

A 1990 U.S. Department of Commerce study of twelve cutting-edge technologies deemed vital to future economic prosperity (superconductors, biotechnology, etc.) concluded that in terms of global competition, the United States was "losing badly" to Japan in four of the technologies, "losing" in six, "holding" in two, and "gaining" in none.[42] Meanwhile, the U.S. was also slipping in another key area of technological capacity, namely patents. An analysis of patents that compared the technical strengths of 1,100 companies around the world revealed that Japan, despite its much smaller industrial base than the United States, nearly closed the gap in total technical strength between 1983 and 1989. The study found that Japan was "continuing to expand in virtually every area of technology."[43] Looking at patents granted in the United States between 1980 and 1990, the trend is unmistakable: eight of the top ten patent winners in 1980 were American firms, only one was Japanese; a decade later, Japanese firms gained five of the top ten positions, American firms only three.[44]

But while much of the U.S. political economy stagnated under Reagan and Bush, eroding its international competitiveness, a number of firms producing for the global market moved in the opposite direction—recording growing sales and increased profits. The value of U.S. exports increased from $201 billion in 1985 to $421.6 billion in 1991; the volume of U.S.-manufactured exports rose by 90% compared with an average 25% in the other OECD countries between 1986 and 1991; and America's share of the industrialized world's manufactured exports jumped from 14% in 1987 to 18% in 1990.[45]

Among the capital goods sectors contributing most to this new "dynamism" of U.S. overseas capital were chemicals, steel, aircraft engines, computers, industrial machinery, military equipment, and consumer goods. In 1991, the computer giant Hewlett-Packard's overseas revenues reached almost 60% of total sales; Pall Corporation, an industrial filter maker, increased its exports to Europe and Asia by 18% and 31% respectively compared to a rise of only 8% in domestic sales; and 80% of Boeing's orders came from foreign airlines. During the same 12-month period, U.S. electronics firms sold $16.1 billion more goods to Western Europe than the latter sold to American customers.[46] One of the biggest turnabouts was in semiconductor sales by U.S. firms, which rose from a 39.2% global market share in 1986 to just over 43% in 1992—approximately equal with Japan although still well below the 1981 peak of 48.9%.[47] Meanwhile, U.S. military contractors' weapons sales abroad nearly quadrupled from $6.5 billion in 1987 to more than $24 billion in 1992—with the Bush administration's aggressive support as evidenced by a 1990 State Department memo circulated to all American embassies "urging all personnel to 'get on board' and help 'open doors' for American weapons export firms."[48] Nonetheless, these various gains need to be kept in perspective: In 1991, export growth accounted for only 7.5% of U.S. economic activity compared with 13.5% for Japan and a phenomenal 28% for Germany.[49]

In the manufacturing sector, increases in productivity, profits, and global market share were accompanied by massive job losses and substantial reductions in workers' wage levels. Seeking to rebound from losses to Japanese competitors totalling around $1 billion in the early 1980s, Caterpillar Inc. shut down nine of its U.S. plants, slashed wages, eliminated thousands of jobs, purchased more parts from outside sellers, doubled the size of its production line, and invested $1.4 billion in a factory modernization program. Between 1980 and 1990, 30,000 employees were sacked but productivity levels increased and sales jumped by 33%. The essential point is that deindustrialization of the American economy is not incompatible with selective reindustrialization, typically linked to high-technology developments whether the example is an individual firm (Caterpillar) or the steel industry which produced an estimated 11.5% of the world's steel in 1990, an increase of 1.2% over 1986.[50]

Those U.S. international export firms that are competitive largely benefit from the declining wages of labor, the high levels of exploitation (extended work days, greater productivity) the shift in social payments from employers to wage earners, the sharp reduction in corporate taxes, and the cheapening of the dollar. The growth of U.S. international capital is paid for, in the first instance, by American factory workers and in general by society at large. The increased hours worked, the sharp decline in social benefits, and the growing use of regressive social taxes (social security) to finance the deficits resulting from tax incentives to capital produces the pattern of declining living standards and the growth of U.S. corporate export sales and profits.

Furthermore, this "export boom" is quite deceptive as an indicator of the revival of U.S. economic power on a global scale because it was partly based on the declining value of the dollar which made U.S. goods cheaper to the more powerful European and Japanese currencies. The Bush administration deliberately pursued a cheap foreign exchange rate strategy to increase America's competitive position abroad. This was what New York investment banker Jeffrey Garten described as a "low wage, commodity intensive" economic vision compared with Japan and Germany where the emphasis is on the quality of their exports. "There is no precedent in history," Garten observed, "where a major industrial power has been competitive while its currency was depreciating."[51]

Even though certain high-tech exports remain globally competitive, America's "leading sectors" in the New World Order are increasingly concentrated among consumer goods firms (Proctor and Gamble, Philip Morris, Johnson and Johnson), the so-called mass entertainment business, construction engineering, clothing apparel (sales to Japan increased from $65 million in 1987 to $400 million in 1991), and the fast food industry.[52]

These "leading sectors," however, are more characteristic of declining powers than ascending hegemons. In the medium term, if the Japanese are eating U.S. hamburgers while the U.S. are buying

Japanese transport and electronics that are at the frontiers of techno-logical advancement, the future power configuration will be sharply at variance with the present. More importantly, listing the successful export corporations avoids the problem of the general decline of the domestic U.S. economy and the fact that many export firms depend heavily on imports from abroad. Furthermore, even the leading services like the entertainment business which shows up as American has come under Japanese or European control in recent years; SONY bought Columbia Pictures for $3.4 billion; Toshiba and Itoh pur-chased a significant part of Time-Warner; Matsushita Electrical Industrial acquired MCA, the owner of Universal Studios, for over $6 billion.

Nor does the growth of U.S. services overseas bolster the ascending hegemon argument. For instance, 7-Eleven convenience stores have spread throughout Japan but the parent company is now locally owned; likewise with the "American" clothing firm, Talbots, which has captured a growing part of the Japanese market in recent years. Even the highly profitable McDonald's in Japan is 50% locally owned. The proliferation of U.S. brands does mean economic power.[53]

Nonetheless, powerful Western media advocates of free markets and deregulated economies such as the *Economist* and the *Wall Street Journal* have displayed a continuing propensity to puff up America's competitive position abroad, all the while ignoring key indicators trending in the opposite direction. The overall decline in U.S. industrial and high-technology competitiveness is, in large part, a result of low levels of research and development (R&D) spending by corporations and the state in comparison with their European and Japanese counterparts. Japanese spending on indus-trial research during the 1980s expanded so rapidly that it equalled or surpassed the United States in this field. In 1989, a U.S. presidential advisory committee on semiconductors attributed Japan's widening lead to the fact that its private sector increased R&D spending at a rate three times that of American computer chip companies. Be-tween 1989 and 1990, Japanese industry increased its R&D spending by 24% in construction, 32% in plastic products, 14% in manufacturing, 11.5% in precision machinery, and by much higher figures in a range of other areas. At the end of the decade, it was spending two-thirds more on R&D in such cutting-edge industries as advanced ceramics.[54]

A report prepared by the National Science Board showed conclusively that industrial R&D in the United States stagnated during the Reagan/Bush years in stark contrast to that of its major capitalist bloc competitors. In the three-year period 1989 to 1991, civilian R&D research in Japan, Germany, France, Italy, Sweden, and Britain cumulatively increased from being 25% to 34% larger than similar activity in the United States. The report noted that U.S. spending slowed from an annual average growth of 7.5% in constant dollars during 1980 to 1985 to only 0.4% between 1985 and 1991.[55]

Civilian R&D spending as a percentage of Gross National Product (GNP) further illustrates the growing gap between the U.S. and its two most formidable capitalist world competitors:

	1978	1980	1984	1986	1988
Japan	2.0	2.2	2.6	2.6	2.9
Germany	2.1	2.3	2.5	2.6	2.7
U.S.	1.6	1.5	1.8	1.8	1.9

This trend showed no signs of reversal in subsequent years: indeed, by 1991 the gap between Japan and the United States had even slightly increased.[56]

While U.S. government non-defense R&D spending (annual average as a percentage of GNP) declined from 0.6% in 1973–81 to 0.4% in 1982–93, federal R&D allocations for defense went in the opposite direction. During the 1978 to 1988 period, it nearly doubled; in 1987, for instance, more than two-thirds of federal government R&D funds ($42 billion out of $60 billion) went into defense-related activities.[57]

Japan's leadership in industrial R&D research has also extended to related fields. With a population around half America's size, and an economy only two-thirds as big, Japan invested more capital in new factories and equipment in 1989 and 1990. Currently, Japan invests over 30% of its Gross Domestic Product (GDP) in assets that produce wealth compared with a U.S. figure of around 17%.[58] Indicators of Japan's growing technological superiority abound: its firms allocate almost double the share of total project costs to tooling and equipment compared to American firms in developing new products and processes; it uses numerically controlled machine tools at one and a half times the U.S. rate; it employs about seven times as many industrial robots per thousand workers as does the U.S.; 93% of its steel is continuously cast compared to only 60% for the world's remaining "superpower."[59] Of course, in the case of industrial robots, their increased use in the U.S. context of unregulated capitalism, where no industrial planning operates to relocate and train displaced workers, will only serve to exacerbate unemployment and heighten social inequalities.

If trade, investment, and market share of high-tech products are indicators of the shift in imperial market power, and reflections of the underlying structural capabilities of each system, so too are levels of foreign aid. In 1988, Japan overtook the United States as the world's largest foreign aid donor and has maintained its leadership ever since. Because most of its overseas development assistance (ODA) is in the form of tied loans and grants for the purchase of Japanese equipment and technology, or for infrastructure and industrial projects from which U.S. (and European) firms are largely excluded, it serves to consolidate Japan's dominance in international markets over the long term.[60]

The rising power of the German mark and Japanese yen vis a vis the U.S. dollar and significantly higher savings rates in Germany and Japan over the past decade or more provide additional evidence of America's declining global position. The share of U.S. dollar holdings of foreign exchange in Central Banks or Treasury Departments fell by 19% between 1975 and 1989 while that of the mark increased by 13% and the yen by 7.4%. In 1989, International Monetary Fund member states kept 20% less of their foreign exchange reserves in dollars than they had in 1975. Another indicator of currency strength is the extent to which Central Banks use it to intervene in exchange markets. Since the late 1970s, the German mark has well and truly displaced the U.S. dollar as the favored central banks' currency for intervening in the European Monetary System. Between 1979 and 1982, it only accounted for 24% of such interventions compared with 72% in dollars; by 1986–87, the roles had almost been reversed with the mark now accounting for 59% of the monies used and the dollar just 26%.[61]

In the area of savings, the finance-speculator capital-based U.S. economy of the 1980s seriously lagged behind the more productive, capital-goods-based economies of Germany and Japan. As a percentage of disposable income, the 1980–88 personal savings rate averages for Germany (12.2) and Japan (16.4) were two and three times greater (respectively) than the U.S. figure (5.5).[62] While the Joint Economic Committee calculated the U.S. figure at a marginally higher 6.57% (1979–89), it pointed out that Americans saved less in the 1980s than in the 1970s.[63] During the Bush presidency, the gap between the United States and its competitor allies, substantial as it already was, actually widened. European economies currently save about two and a half times, and Japan around five times, as much as the American economy.[64]

As the global power battlefield shifts from military and ideological competition to markets, investment, and high-technology production, countries such as Germany and Japan will be much better positioned to launch new lines of innovative goods and services in the future, increasingly at the expense of the United States, thereby providing these economies with powerful weapons in the trade wars of the 1990s. In the absence of any sustained effort to contract its noneconomic overhead expenses (military, etc.), the manifest internal weaknesses of American capitalism relative to its competitor allies looms larger than ever. What is indisputable, however, is that a restructuring process has taken place over the past decade—based on compradore and speculator capital, consumer imports, and overseas loans to finance debts and deficits "pushing out" savings and investment in productive activity, and the export of finished goods— which has transformed the U.S. from an industrial imperial empire to a "tributary" imperial power.

The long-term, large-scale effects of this shift were particularly evident in developments within the service sector. Although accounting for almost all the new jobs created and more than two-thirds of the increase in GNP in the two decades prior to 1990, the sector's productivity growth rate remained stagnant throughout the 1970s and 1980s. Between 1948 and 1973, the average annual rate of productivity increase was 2.5%; from 1973 to 1987, it declined to 0.7%. When combined with the growth of the speculative economy, it is not surprising that these figures were replicated in terms of overall productivity levels in the United States during these same periods (from 3% to 0.9%).[65] Comparisons with Japan and Germany are instructive: between 1975 and 1988, the cumulative percentage of productivity growth in Japan (49) was more than four times that of the U.S. (11); between 1982 and 1991, productivity in Japan increased at an average annual rate of 3%, in Germany at just under 2%, and in the United States at little more than 1%.[66] Such figures underscore the basic incompatibility between long-term productivity increases and the predominance of speculative investments.

America's global decline, brought about in large part by the structural weakness of the domestic economy, has undermined Washington's ability to effectively participate in the competition among the leading capitalist powers to establish spheres of influence in countries of the former Soviet empire. Possessing Europe's most advanced and dynamic industrial-technical infrastructure, Germany, not the United States, has emerged as the leading external power in these economies, especially in the trade sphere. Between 1985 and 1988, it captured 30% of these markets; its share of the industrialized West's total exports to the Soviet bloc countries increased from 17% to 21% while Japan's rose marginally to about 10%, and the United States lagged behind, its share having fallen slightly to less than 7%.[67] By the end of the decade, Germany controlled 45% of Eastern Europe's machine tool market compared to less than 2% for the United States.[68] And precisely because it is exporting large quantities of capital goods (as well as clothing and textiles), the aggregate statistics probably understate Germany's potential to establish itself as the long-term regional economic power.

European, and especially German, firms also surged ahead of the United States (and Japan) in the foreign investment area. By

1992, Germany had established itself as the leading foreign investor in Poland and Czechoslovakia and, in the view of a knowledgeable American investment banker, this domination was likely to spread through the former bloc countries: "They'll have an automatic 'in' in the old Soviet Union and Eastern Europe because they will be the suppliers of the capital goods."[69] Germany's estimated $40 billion in loans, grants, and credits to these countries during the early 1990s, at least five times the amount provided by Washington, seemed likely to consolidate this advantage. The noticeable absence of significant long-term, large-scale U.S. investment in the former Soviet bloc has been attributed by some commentators to Washington's foot-dragging on providing the necessary investment guarantees. But this ignores other, more important factors including overseas investors' preferences for quick profits.

A recent two-year study commissioned by the Harvard Business School and the Council on Competitiveness "marshalled some fairly compelling evidence to support the contention that American managers do make fewer long-term investments than their peers in Japan or Europe." Included in the study was a global survey of around 300 large companies which found that 61% of the Europeans' investment projects were long term (i.e., no profits expected for the first five years) compared to 47% for the Japanese and only 21% for the Americans.[70] In other words, U.S. capitalism's major economic competitors commit two to three times as much of their investment funds to long-term undertakings. This "making money" rather than "making goods" mentality is further testimony to the hegemony of the speculator in the late-twentieth-century American political economy.

U.S. capitalism's reluctance to make long-term investments also extends to the training of productive labor. Japanese and European managers spent three to five times as much during the 1980s to upgrade worker skills, thus ensuring a greater commitment to quality production.[71] U.S. industry currently spends only two-thirds the amount outlayed by Japanese and German corporations for worker training, and the bulk of these funds are invested in the professional and managerial staffs, not the "front-line" workers.[72] Japanese capital has also encouraged and sponsored its scientists to study abroad to a far greater degree than American corporations. Keeping such close tabs on global technological advances enables Japanese firms to much more rapidly convert the new technologies into marketable export products.

The emergence of Japan as an economic powerhouse during the 1970s and 1980s has been attributed in large part to the greater technical and scientific literacy of its blue-collar workforce. One specialist on this topic explained: "[They] can interpret advanced mathematics, read complex engineering blue-prints, and perform sophisticated tasks on the factory floor far better than blue collars in the U.S."[73] There is plenty of evidence to support this conclusion, not least the fact that over the past twenty years the test scores in math and science of American students have consistently lagged behind those of students in Japan (and a number of other European countries).[74] Higher educational institutions in the United States have also contributed to the skills gap. Whereas in the 1950s and 1960s, the heyday of U.S. global economic power, the number of advanced engineering degrees exceeded Masters of Business Administration (MBA) degrees, since those years the trend has been reversed—coinciding with the steady erosion of the country's manufacturing base. In the 1970s, there were more than twice as many MBA graduates; in the 1980s, the gap actually widened as business schools churned out over 64,000 graduates compared to just 20,000 new graduates produced by the nation's engineering faculties. Worse still, many of the latter were foreign nationals who subsequently returned to their country of origin. By contrast, in 1989 alone, Japanese universities awarded nearly 12,000 advanced engineering degrees and only 1,000 MBAs.[75] A recent OECD report notes that American universities still lag from 7 to 10 percent behind their Japanese and German counterparts in the number of degrees awarded annually in science and engineering.[76]

Another worker skills area that has a low priority within the U.S. corporate sector compared to its major global competitors is that of vocational training programs. The most striking contrast is with Germany which, with only a quarter of the population, has almost six times as many apprenticeships (1.7 million vs. less than 300,000).[77] The reason is not difficult to find. Germany's vocational training system is based on a high degree of cooperation between the peak business associations and a powerful trade union movement in "defining the school curriculum and job qualifications for a large number of occupations and trades." And the state acts as the backstop and legitimator of the process, "sanction[ing] as public policy the agreements hammered out by the various groups."[78] In the United States neither of these factors have been operative: capital and the state have not developed a significant cooperative relationship regarding this issue, and organized labor is so weak that it is almost totally excluded from decision making about investment or employment, both at the level of individual firms and nationally.

The educational and worker training orientation of Japanese and German industrial (and financial) capital offers a sharp contrast to the behavior and commitments of the American banking and industrial capitalist class—reflecting the different roles they play (expanding vs. pillaging industry) in the national economy. In February 1992, the Japanese Prime Minister Kiichi Miyazawa criticized American capitalism for its attitude toward education, its reluctance to make long-term investments, its responsibility for declining worker skills, and the "making money, not goods" approach. "Looking at what things have come to in the past 10 years," he perceptively observed,

> "we might say that the interpretation of producing or creating value has become very loose [in the United States]. . . . People graduating from universities are going to Wall Street for high salaries. As a result, the number of engineers who actually make things is shrinking. While [there was] debate whether this is all right or not, the money markets advanced and junk bonds appeared—junk bonds, just as the name applies; very dangerous. We have leveraged buyouts, where those without their own money can buy things and then, unable to pay interest on the debts, fall into bankruptcy. It should be obvious to anyone that such a situation could not continue for long."[79]

In the savage, and largely irrelevant, U.S. media response that followed, the basic thrust of his comments were all but ignored.

THE TWO-TRACK ECONOMY: U.S.
ECONOMIC EXPANSION ABROAD

The central paradox of the Reagan-Bush era (and continuing to the present day) is that while the U.S. "national economy" declined, and notwithstanding the ebbing of U.S. global economic power relative to its major capitalist competitors, America's overseas economic actors (even more so than locally based exporters) revealed an increasing capacity to expand and maximize profits. The growth of the international circuits of U.S. transnational corporations (TNCs), facilitated by state subsidies and diversion of more and more corporate resources to global activities, in turn created a progressively wider gap between the accumulation needs of these circuits and the (budget and trade) interests of nationally anchored political and corporate decision makers. This fuelled a spiralling tension between the national state's commitment to an expanding U.S. private global empire and the requirements of large-scale domestic capital. This tension was further exacerbated by a number of other factors. Some TNCs involved in global markets, for instance, opposed anti-dumping laws prohibiting foreign firms from selling goods in the U.S. market below production costs in order to promote their own export interests. Others, wanting to license and sell technologies to Japan and Europe for their immediate gain, triggered conflicts with elected officials seeking to retain national technological and competitive advantages. Of equal concern to these politicians was the fact that many TNCs paid low or negative taxes at home, thus contributing to the rising U.S. budget deficit. IBM, for example, paid negative federal income taxes in 1986 and 1987 as a result of deductions claimed for R&D spending related to its foreign operations.[80]

In the search for markets, technology, and lower productive costs, U.S. direct overseas investment has grown at a faster rate than the domestic economy over the past twenty years. And despite a steady decline in global share since 1960, it has also grown more rapidly in absolute terms than Japanese and German foreign investment since the mid-1980s: from $361.6 billion in 1984 to $665.3 billion in 1991. This sustained "pull" of global sites over the home economy testifies precisely to a greater ability to maximize profits abroad: between 1982 and 1991, the foreign profits of American TNCs rose at a compound annual rate (10.8%) almost twice as fast as their domestic profits.[81]

According to the U.S. Department of Commerce, the majority-owned affiliates of American TNCs increased their capital expenditures by an annual average of 19% between 1987 ($34.4 billion) and 1990 ($61.2 billion). The most dramatic growth occurred in manufacturing affiliates that increased their capital spending by around 70% from $17.2 billion to $29.4 billion. In 1990 alone, U.S. manufacturing firms launched 271 new projects abroad, a 25% increase over 1989. During this same four-year period, domestic capital spending by all U.S. businesses grew, on average, by only 9%. Although the rate of capital spending by all majority-owned affiliates in 1991 and 1992 fell as a result of a declining need for new overseas capacity and stagnation in the United States and global economies, it still topped the rate of growth of national private investment.[82]

Any number of examples illustrate this investment pattern: between 1985 and 1987, Ford Motor Company raised its capital expenditures in Europe by 37% while its spending on domestic operations fell by 17%; between 1989 and 1992, a California computer disk drives firm, Connor Peripherals, hired 7,100 new workers, almost all of whom (6,945) were employed in its overseas affiliates; seven of the last ten investment commitments made by the Du Pont Company, each over $100 million, have been in Europe and Asia. R&D spending by American corporations exhibits a similar trend.[83] The National Science Foundation reported that between 1985 and 1987, spending by foreign affiliates of TNCs grew at a robust 35%. During approximately the same period, firms' domestic R&D spending rose by a meager 6%.[84] Other figures deepen the contrast and underscore the relationship between the lack of domestic investment, rising unemployment, declining living standards, and national economic decay. In the 1980s, for instance, the capital stock per worker (equipment plus buildings) rose by only 8.7% compared to 14.1% in the 1970s. Taking the amount of equipment alone, the situation is even worse—the growth rate declined to just over one-third. In 1991, net business investment dropped to 0.9% of Gross Domestic Product (GDP), the lowest figure in more than three decades—reflecting the continuing preference for sacking workers, not increasing investment in machines and equipment, in efforts to generate productivity growth.[85]

While American economists and political leaders complain interminably about the lack of investment in capital expenditures and R&D, and scurry around blaming U.S. consumers, the reality is that American corporations do invest in both in increasing amounts—abroad. This trend has been actively promoted and facilitated by U.S. governmental and state institutions, most notably in the Central American/Caribbean area—with attendant devastating consequences for the national economy.

The Bush administration's support for the North American Free Trade Association (NAFTA) was accompanied by repeated statements that the program would create large numbers of new jobs in the United States and not encourage domestic firms to relocate to Mexico to take advantage of manufacturing wage levels that averaged around 15% of U.S. wages, and were even less in other sectors. But, in fact, the contrary has occurred: between 1987 and 1991, U.S. companies invested $11.6 billion in Mexican plants, attracted by the low wages that would enable them to produce cheap, high-quality goods and thus become more globally competitive. Such investments have not been confined to assembly plants (maquiladoras) but have seen TNCs such as Ford Motor Company establish full-scale factories in Mexico. As a result, while manufacturing jobs in Mexican-based affiliates increased by almost 25% between 1986 and 1990, manufacturing jobs in the U.S. domestic economy rose by less than 1%.[86]

A 1992 study by economists Timothy Keochlin and Mehrene Larudee concluded that NAFTA could be expected to divert as much as $53 billion in new U.S. investment over this decade, taking advantage of low-wage labor while still being able to produce for the American market.[87] The "pull" of the former is indisputable, both in absolute terms and even relative to other Third World locations. The average hourly wage for U.S. factory workers compared to their Mexican counterparts was decisive in the August 1992 announcement by the Smith Corona Corporation that it was moving its manufacturing operations south: $18 (including fringe benefits and factory supervisor compensation) vs. less than $4.00.[88] Some months earlier, the American-owned transnational Zenith closed its manufacturing operations in Taiwan where the average hourly wage was $4.10 and shifted to Mexico to further maximize profits—based on paying its workers there only $2.03 per hour.[89] Apart from a major diversion of U.S. investment to Mexico, the Keochlin-Larudee study projected the disappearance of an estimated 290,000 to 490,000 jobs and the cumulative loss of as much as $320 billion in U.S. wage income by the year 2000.[90]

Under Reagan and Bush, the U.S. government, through the Agency for International Development (AID), channeled more than $1.3 billion into Central American and Caribbean trade associations, chambers of commerce, and investment promotion organizations with the stated objective of encouraging U.S. manufacturing firms to move their operations to these low-wage areas. In El Salvador, for example, AID pumped more than $102 million into a private development organization, FUSADES, between 1984 and the early 1990s. The 1991 agreement with FUSADES called for "a proactive, direct and systematic sales effort involving direct contact with targeted U.S. firms to convince them to explore opportunities in El Salvador. . . . The industry focus will largely be apparel but could also include electronics/electrical assembly and other labor-intensive assembly activities."[91]

The success of these Reagan/Bush efforts to build "export processing zones" in the Central American/Caribbean Basin had a massive impact on the U.S. domestic economy: thousands of lost jobs, wage cuts for hundreds of thousands of workers, and a general deterioration in factory work conditions amid the constant threat of additional sackings. From 1990 to late 1992, thirty U.S. apparel manufacturers shifted their operations to El Salvador, Guatemala, and Honduras while an additional sixty-eight had their products made in these three countries. For workers in the U.S. clothing industry, these developments were predictably catastrophic: fifty-eight plant closures and 12,000 job layoffs.[92]

During the 1980s, Republican presidents and Democratic-controlled legislatures combined to produce a trade policy, under the banner of "global competitiveness," that overwhelmingly benefitted the international operations of American TNCs. While U.S.-produced manufactured exports declined as a percentage of world total, sales by foreign-based affiliates of these same American-based corporations increased significantly. Their share of total OECD exports increased from 14% in 1983 to 19% in 1989. American corporations produced around 20% of their output overseas while the equivalent figure for their Japanese counterparts was around 5%.[93]

By the early 1990s, most of America's transnational corporations were primarily dependent for their sales, production, and profits on their international circuits. Sales by foreign non-bank affiliates of these transnationals on a worldwide basis totalled more than $1 trillion annually, four times the value of nationally produced merchandise exports.[94] In Europe, for instance, U.S.-based producers sell about $70 billion worth of products annually, which is less than 15% of the value of goods sold in the EEC by locally based affiliates of American TNCs ($500 billion). The experience of General Motors signified this growing ascendancy of the international circuits: after losing $2.3 billion between 1980 and 1986, General Motors-Europe increased its sales by over 60% in the next five years, recording a 1991 profit of $1.8 billion. In 1992, the affiliate's parts sales rose an estimated 18% to $4 billion. The parent company in Detroit, meanwhile, lost $4.5 billion in 1991 alone.[95] This commitment of General Motors and other U.S. transnationals to operate within Europe means that "home country" efforts to increase the levels of merchandise exports in order to reduce the national trade deficit does not bode well for the future. This is especially so against the background of growing European economic integration that is certain to make it more difficult for U.S. exports to enter the continent.

The whole debate about U.S. "stagnation" and "decline," and the various prescriptions put forth to overcome these problems, takes on a radically different appearance if it is located within the context of the TNC-U.S. national state relationship. First, insofar as the TNCs are "part of the U.S.," these socioeconomic units are not stagnating or declining. Unlike the national state and the vast majority of U.S. wage, salaried, and self-employed workers not linked to the international circuits (to which this thesis does apply), these "external" units are growing and expanding. Second, it is completely incorrect to attribute stagnation in the domestic economy to low levels of investment in capital equipment and R&D, and to unsatisfactory public and private savings rates. The key to diagnosing the problem is not the lack of investment or savings but identifying the site or regional locus of such activity. As we have shown, American TNCs invest and save primarily within their international circuits. Prescriptions to stimulate growth that focus on capital gains taxes and other incentives, insofar as they are tied to the TNC, will only hasten and deepen their international linkages while further depriving the domestic economy of funds for social expenditure and public investments. In other words, given the present-day structure of U.S. capitalism, more state subsidies to large outward-oriented corporations will only extend the gap between global empire and domestic decay.

The clarion calls by professional economists and politicians for greater efforts to make the U.S. more globally competitive and domestically prosperous are simply yodelling in the Rockies. If the last decade or so demonstrates anything at all it is that the conditions for promoting the former are diametrically opposed to achieving the latter. Only by fundamentally restructuring or dismantling capital (neither likely propositions) can new sites and circuits for the production of goods and services for the vast majority of Americans become possible. It is unreasonable to expect a return to the period when private U.S. corporations operated principally within the boundaries of the "home state." Nor is there any likelihood that a national industrial policy will emerge from political parties beholden to TNCs who are so deeply entrenched in their international circuits. The global marketplace orientation of the TNCs undermine efforts to divert resources to the U.S. domestic market and socioeconomic reforms. Because the TNCs have such a great need for overseas profits, they have profoundly influenced state policy such that it focuses almost exclusively on sustaining international circuits and the conditions for external growth. The TNCs' dominant position within the U.S. state has ensured the absence of almost any restrictive policy and reaffirmed the dominant ethos of "globalism"—an ideology that permeates all segments of the political spectrum in the United States today.

In the era of the New World Order, the U.S. state diverts resources from the national enemy, favors speculative over productive capital, and provides incentives that promote the growth of U.S. overseas capital. Thus, as the imperial economy grows, the domestic economy disintegrates. Nevertheless, as the internal crisis accompanying global expansion deepens, it provokes a more profound malaise that has recently found expression in both demagogic, chauvinistic appeals by the ultra-right and vacuous populist sloganeering by the left of the Democratic Party. However, since neither has any desire to confront the power and influence of the TNCs within the national state, these policy positions will have no more impact or consequence than prior critiques of a similar kind. Only a major popular upheaval stemming from an even more severe collapse of living standards and the emergence of a new national anticorporate movement can pose the issue of global empire versus domestic rebirth.

THE USES OF JAPANESE BASHING: WASHINGTON'S STRATEGY FOR THE 1990s

While American transnational corporations have increased their investments, export sales, and profits in recent years, their global percentages and market shares have simultaneously declined in both Asia and Europe. The greatest gains have been made by the Japanese, especially in Asia where they have effectively displaced the U.S. as the dominant "external" economic power.

Between 1986 and 1991, Japanese transnationals spent more than $25 billion (triple the U.S. figure) to transform Asia "into its manufacturing and merchandising backyard." [96] By 1991, Japanese-direct foreign investment in Southeast Asia ($8.7 billion) was almost double the amount of funds invested by U.S. transnationals ($4.4 billion). [97] In the area of trade, the rise in market share was just as dramatic: between 1985 and 1990, Japan's share of Southeast Asian imports increased at almost double the rate of the increase in the U.S. share (2.7% to 36.5% of the total versus 0.8% to 18.9%). [98] In the automobile sector, Japanese domination is almost total: its companies control about 90% of the market for commercial vehicles and 85% for passenger cars while U.S. companies have a less than 1% share. In fact, in most Asian markets today, Detroit's "Big Three" automobile producers "are little more than niche players." This even includes the Philippines, the only Asian country where right-hand side of the road driving operates, whose market has been almost totally captured by the major Japanese transnationals. [99]

Although relatively less prominent in Europe, the Japanese have nonetheless managed to establish a powerful capital and commercial presence since the mid-1980s, offering a formidable challenge to U.S. efforts to gain a major foothold inside the EEC. Japanese-direct foreign investment in Europe increased from $1.9 billion in 1985 to $14.8 billion in 1989. By the end of the decade, there were approximately 500 factories with at least 10% Japanese equity. Tokyo's investment strategy was based on seeking the most favorable terrain: the largest amount of capital found a home in Thatcher's "free market" England. [100] The growth in Japanese trade has been equally impressive: exports to the European Community increased from $30.7 billion in 1986 to $53.6 billion in 1990, contributing to an annual average trade surplus over $19.5 billion. In 1991, this surplus jumped to $27.4 billion. [101] By comparison, the U.S. gains were far more limited (from a trade deficit of $16.6 billion in 1987 to a surplus of $17 billion in 1991). [102] If it were not for the imposition of quotas, the levelling of dumping charges, and increased funding of local high-tech industries by European governments, Japanese market share and profits in automobiles, computers, consumer electronics, semiconductors, etc. would have been even greater.

The concentrated targeting of Japan is a central element of U.S.

global economic strategy in the 1990s. The strategy has three interrelated objectives: first, to accelerate the growth of U.S. capital overseas, further depriving the domestic economy of funding resources; second, to exploit the mass media as a means of diverting popular discontent toward external competitors as the source of internal deterioration, thereby shifting responsibility away from the U.S. state and corporations; and third, to use the heightened domestic chauvinism to bludgeon capitalist competitors, especially Japan, into making additional concessions to U.S. international capital in their own markets.

This strategy allows the U.S. corporate elite to gain *politically* by channelling discontent toward external overseas rivals and away from domestic anticorporate movements. It also enables U.S. capital to move abroad in search of new sources of cheap labor (Mexico, Eastern Europe), and greater access to lucrative markets (Europe). The particular strategy that focuses on generating mass anti-Japanese sentiment at home while promoting U.S. transnational activity abroad forces divisions among adversaries. Simultaneously, this artificially created domestic discontent provides Washington with a bargaining tool to extract further concessions for American multinationals and banks desiring entry into the Japanese market.

In a world of rising inter-capitalist competition, U.S. corporate and state elites have opted for a strategy of diverting resources from the domestic economy to secure greater global market shares, thereby deepening the gap between overseas capital gains and domestic living standards. By contrast, the German and Japanese strategy has been oriented toward strengthening the domestic economy as a basis for projecting into world markets and reinvesting earnings gained abroad into the development of nationally anchored, advanced technologies—in the process, limiting the external/internal gap to a much greater degree than in the U.S. There, the cleavage between "externally growing capital" and a downwardly mobile labor force continues to widen, becoming a source of a deepening popular malaise.

The political problem for outwardly oriented capital is to find and promote a political-ideological formula that can channel this discontent *away* from the sources of downward mobility and, if possible, *toward* external economic competitors, imagined or invented political threats, or domestic scapegoats at the bottom of the socioeconomic ladder.

The centerpiece of the effort to externalize the domestic malaise has taken the form of a heightened campaign against Japanese political leaders, economic policies, and cultural practices. The growth of Japanese trade and investment networks outcompeting their American counterparts has encouraged U.S. policymakers to present a distorted and falsified version of Japan's critique of U.S. capitalism in order to fashion an effective ideological weapon with which to generate mass chauvinist hostility toward a competitor ally. Washington has warned Japanese leaders to cease criticizing U.S. capital in that area where it is most politically vulnerable: its "making money over goods" approach—its channelling of massive profits, labor givebacks, capital tax reductions, and other state concessions into speculative activity at home and funding an expanding "empire" abroad.

American politicians and media analysts have consistently attributed the nation's chronic trade deficit with Japan (running at between $40 billion and $50 billion annually since the mid-1980s) to the latter's closed market, high tariffs, import restrictions, or bureaucratic impediments to market access. But as Stephen Cohen observes, taking natural resources, geographic location, and other specific features of Japan's economic circumstances into account, quantitative studies provide no evidence to support the "unfair trade" and "anti-worker" assertions.[103] Empirically, a number of assertions are simply wrong; little more than propaganda ploys. First, while there are still tariff barriers against selected agricultural imports such as rice, all tariffs and quotas against manufactured imports have been virtually eliminated. Second, Japan's tariffs today are among the lowest in the world. Third, the country's trade bureaucracy, MITI, now actively promotes, not discourages, sales of foreign products in the domestic economy. In 1991, the government offered tax credits to local companies that increased their volume of imports as well as low-interest financing for overseas firms that export to Japan.[104] Despite U.S. complaints about lack of market access, the reality is that foreign corporations have substantially increased their presence in the Japanese market since the latter half of the 1980s. Between 1986 and 1988, for instance, the value of manufactured imports almost doubled from $44 billion to $85.6 billion.[105]

The problems confronting American TNCs seeking to enter the Japanese market are largely self-inflicted: a failure to adapt to market needs, a short-term investment perspective, low levels of R&D spending, etc. The stance of the U.S. automobile transnationals is particularly illuminating. While European car markets have adapted to Japanese tastes and habits, and made long-term investments geared to the domestic market, Detroit's "Big Three" invest in Japanese car manufacturers primarily to produce parts or automobiles that can be sold in the U.S. Both Chrysler, which owns nearly 11% of the Mitsubishi Motors Corporation, and General Motors, which has a stake in Isuzu Motors, have largely squandered opportunities to break into the local market; only Ford has arranged with its local partner, Mazda Motor, to produce cars for domestic sale (with the steering wheel on the right-hand side). Moreover, Ford is the only one of the "Big Three" that has taken a lead from the two most successful foreign automobile companies in Japan, Mercedez-Benz and BMW, and established its own local dealership.[106]

Apart from repeated attacks on Japan for playing the international trade game by "unfair rules," Washington and the mass media have focused on allegations of political corruption within the Japanese elite and the tight links between business and the state, accompanied by an emphasis in Japanese society on racial purity—the racist character of the potential "conqueror."[107] This diffuse propaganda serves a number of purposes. By casting Japanese society and people in a very negative light—corrupt and oppressive at home—it suggests that by extension they would behave the same overseas when they establish positions of power. The negative imagery and sensibility generated among the U.S. public can be tapped whenever the occasion warrants—when and if, for example, a new wave of discontent with American corporate practices surfaces or unemployment rises dramatically. In recent years, the White House, legislators, and corporate executives have all sought to focus the popular mind on

Japanese "expansionism" in the domestic economy. The aims are not difficult to identify. Such a strategy can serve the purpose of distracting from U.S. global "empire building" initiatives or rationalize these large-scale diversions of resources overseas as necessary to maintain "global competitiveness."

It is of course quite easy to dispose of these propaganda ploys: Japanese corporations do not practice racism in hiring employees; Japan is not the leading foreign investor in the United States; Japanese purchases of U.S. Treasury notes fund approximately one-third of the nation's budget deficit; between 1988 and 1992, Japan shifted from a net investor in U.S. government securities to the tune of $30.7 billion in 1988 to a net seller in 1992. Since 1990, new investment outlays have plummeted by around 75%, due largely to a combination of overpriced purchases in the past (e.g., Sony and Matsushita's splurges in Hollywood), falling profits, and, increasingly, substantial losses. The Rockefeller Center is now estimated to be worth less than the Japanese purchase price, which may explain why total real estate investments tumbled from $13 billion in 1990 to $5 billion in 1991. In the twelve months up to March 1992, affiliates of Japanese companies operating in North America suffered combined losses of around $1.5 billion.[108] In a word, Japan is neither "taking over" the U.S. economy nor imposing alien cultural practices. A more reasonable and judicious account would probably credit Tokyo with helping to bolster the sagging U.S. economy hit hard by large-scale capital flight. But the logic of the U.S. propaganda war with Japan is not found in a rational assessment of how the two economies are articulated; the key is the *internal* structural contradictions of the U.S. political economy.

Elite-cultivated chauvinism reflects the deepening gap between the power and growth of U.S. capital in the international economy and the downward spiral of living and working conditions affecting America's working people. Inherent in that contradiction is an enduring need to constantly invent external enemies: capitalist competitors being only one of many possibilities. Another type of "adversary" confronted throughout the 1980s (and into the 1990s) was found in the Third World, where the U.S. propaganda machine created "threats," demonized political antagonists, sanitized wars of intervention, all the while mesmerizing public opinion.

Nor are external enemies the sole source for refocusing public discontent with downward mobility. Domestic society has ready adversaries for sustaining links between its economic "losers" and the outwardly expanding corporate elite. The "dirty secret" of the corporate-state elite is to keep the public looking *downward* and *not upward* as a source of their problems. The overall strategy is to put those who have been pushed to the bottom against those who are falling: according to corporate ideologues, taxes from the working and middle classes are linked to social programs for the ex-workers and the ex-middle class, rather than the half-trillion-dollar bail-out of the Savings and Loan institutions. The increasing costs of medical care, the growing social security taxes, and declining employer financial benefits are blamed on unemployed workers, those on food stamps, the aged, the welfare mothers, instead of the wealthy who benefit from capital gains tax reduction and multi-billion-dollar overseas tax write-offs.

The propaganda ploy in this context is to *ethnicize crime*—identify violent crime with blacks, and stigmatize women (feminists) for the disintegrating family and communities—not corporate flight, deindustrialization, or corporate designed technological changes that displace labor, undermine stable employment, and lower living standards. Elite ideologues can invent many more subjects for political exploitation in the domestic economy. Their method is to divorce abstract moral values from concrete economic interests. Moral failings are extrapolated from their state and corporate causes and then falsely attributed to the personal character of other victimized groups.

The growing irrational anti-Japanese campaign thus dovetails with the efforts to find domestic scapegoats, both linked to the widening gap between the global empire of corporate America and domestic decay.

EXTERNAL EXPANSION AND INTERNAL DECAY: THE DIALECTICS OF GLOBAL POWER

Our discussion to date has stressed the U.S. government's willingness to channel large amounts of economic resources abroad to build and bolster its global empire: either directly through subsidies to the overseas transnational class and economic and military assistance programs, or indirectly through wage, labor, and taxation policies favoring the outward-looking investors. And as American corporations increasingly depend on foreign earnings, markets, and assets relative to domestic profits, this generates a built-in pressure to expand imperial state commitments in an ever-deepening cycle—whether they be free-trade agreements in the Western Hemisphere, new foreign aid programs to leverage market openings and resources access for U.S. transnationals in Eastern Europe, or continued military efforts to carve out "space" in the Middle East.

The closure of selected military bases and seaports and other modest cutbacks of this kind are not intended to provide the wherewithal for new domestic investments in the productive or social welfare sectors; rather, they are geared to lowering taxes for potential and actual foreign investors, and increasing U.S. competitiveness abroad. The drive for global supremacy, in its military-ideological form or in some new international or regional bloc framework, remains the core preoccupation of American policymakers.

Increasingly, the achievement of this objective depends upon the shift of domestic resources for use by those private and public actors involved in empire building. The consequences of the sustained diversion of state monies to empire building over the past decade and a half for the U.S. national economy have been catastrophic: deteriorating social programs, disintegrating public health and educational sectors, rising homelessness, worsening unemployment, and spreading poverty. Put another way, the efforts by the country's overseas investor class to sustain high global profits and market share is based on greater wealth concentration and economic inequalities in the domestic sphere. The ability of this class to set or influence state policy priorities and channel the flow of resources to fund their global activities is substantially tied to its already considerable financial power that has allowed it to dominate electoral politics at the national level.

U.S. global empire building is producing a two-tiered "Third World" economy and society at home: the majority of the population linked to a decaying domestic economy, and an elite linked to global networks that grows wealthy on private services and public subsidies. In this chapter, we analyze the consequences of this push to reaffirm dominant world power status and show how it is directly related to the erosion of living and working conditions in the United States. We argue that the state cannot simultaneously maintain a global empire and provide the services and funds so critical to the revival of a more dynamic national economy.

WEALTH CONCENTRATION AND INCOME INEQUALITIES

The depth and scope of domestic disintegration can best be understood by examining a number of critical areas, foremost among which are the twin issues of a growing concentration of capital and a widening gap between the incomes of rich and poor. There is undisputed evidence that living standards for the great majority of American wage workers have fallen over the past twenty years while those in the wealthiest quintile have steadily increased their incomes and the top 1% have reaped even greater financial rewards from activities largely unrelated to productivity.

The processes of economic inequality and social polarization increased dramatically during the Reagan/Bush era. The income of families in the top 1% increased more than 87% and only the top 20% of families saw their share of national income rise; for the middle 20%, the increase was negligible while the income of those families in the lowest quintile declined by 10.4%.[1] Between 1980 and 1989, the combined salaries of middle-income earners ($20,000 to $50,000) increased by 4% annually; those in the $200,000 to $1 million bracket rose by more than 60%; and those receiving in excess of $1 million rose by almost 200%. The income gap between the very rich and the very poor is even more marked: during this same period, the average wage of those earning less than $20,000 a year increased by a paltry 1.4% while those earning over $1 million almost doubled their salaries.[2] The breakdown along race lines is just as stark. In 1987, the average black family's income was around 56% of their white counterpart—the biggest disparity since the 1960s.[3]

What is clear is that it is not just those wage workers in the lowest quintile that have suffered a decline in incomes. Indeed, the share of income held by the middle 20% of American families reached its lowest point in 1990 since the Census Bureau began collecting information in 1947.[4] Furthermore, the gap between rich and poor families would have been even wider had not working mothers in two-parent families labored almost one-third more hours in 1989 than they did in 1979. A Joint Economic Committee study notes that the real hourly pay of husbands in the bottom 60% of two-income families actually fell during the 1980s, and that most of the meager increases in income (in inflation-adjusted dollars) came from additional hours worked, not higher real wages earned.[5]

In contrast to an almost 200% rise in the net worth of the richest 400 Americans between 1982 and 1989, the income of the country's wage workers failed to keep pace even with the 18% Consumer Price Index rise during this period. Indeed, for the first time since mid-century, the average hourly wage (in 1977 dollars) for over 90 million workers fell steadily from $4.89 in 1980 to $4.80 in 1989. The decline continued through the Bush years: real hourly compensation in the fourth quarter of 1991 was no higher than for the last quarter of 1976.[6] But while inflation continued to erode workers' purchasing power, and despite the onset of an increasingly severe recession, executive pay packets spiralled upward. By the end of the 1980s, compensation specialist Grael Crystal estimated that the incomes of the chief executive officers (CEOs) of America's largest corporations were 120 times that of the average worker, a more than tripling of the gap since the mid-1970s.[7] And this income differential continues to widen: in 1991, the average compensation awarded to CEOs of 360 of the country's largest corporations rose by 26% over 1990 compared with a minuscule 2.6% rise in the average earnings of blue- and white-collar workers in the private sector; in 1992, according to *Business Week*, the average CEO salary increased by an extraordinary 56%, more than 200 times the wage of the average worker.[8]

If the income gap between workers and executives in the United States is greater than in most other industrialized countries, so is the income spread between American CEOs and their counterparts in the major capitalist competitor nations. Whereas the former earned incomes averaging around $3.2 million in 1990, German and Japanese executive were paid about $800,000 and $525,000 respectively.[9] And even if stock options and other noncash compensation which account for approximately half of American CEOs' remuneration are excluded, the latter still earn two to three times as much as their European counterparts. Moreover, unlike the Japanese, American chief executives receive continually increasing financial benefits irrespective of the economic health of their corporation. The 1991 compensation increases occurred at a time when, according to studies by Standard & Poor's and the New York consulting firm Towers Perrin, these companies' profit levels were falling sharply. By contrast, in early 1992 the CEOs of Hitachi, Fujitsue, IBM Japan, Japanese Airlines, and the Ricoh Corporation announced cuts in their base pay of between 20% and 35% as a result of major company operating losses.[10]

The Reagan administration presided over an increasing concentration of wealth and income, a trend most strikingly revealed in the fact that between 1983 and 1989 the richest 1% of households increased their share of the private net worth of American families from 31% to 38%.[11] This was largely the result of capital generated by stocks and bonds, real estate, dividends, interest, and other unearned sources—not a consequence of new investments in productive activity. These growing economic inequalities in American life were enormously facilitated by changes to the tax laws. The 1981 tax bill, for instance, raised inheritance tax exemption and gift tax exclusion while lowering maximum real estate taxes. Within five years, "the tax burdens paid primarily by the very wealthy" fell by $4.7 billion.[12] In 1986, Congress passed the Tax Reform Act with its alternative minimum tax provision designed to ensure that everybody paid some monies to the Internal Revenue Service. By 1989, the number of individuals and families paying this alternative minimum tax had dropped from almost 200,000 to 50,000 and the amount they paid dropped from $4.6 billion to a stingy $476,000.[13] The corporate sector share of federal income tax declined from 21% in 1980 to 17% in 1990.[14]

While changes in the tax laws were a massive financial bonanza for the rich and the very rich, they simply accelerated the erosion of living standards for the middle and lower classes. Between 1980 and 1990, the combined effective federal tax rate (income, social security, corporate, excise, etc.) for families in the bottom 20% increased by 16.1%, and in the next two quintiles by 6% and 1.2% respectively. At the same time, it fell by 5.5% for the top 20% and a spectacular 14.4% for the richest 1%.[15] The much vaunted 1986 Tax Reform Act dramatically entrenched this trend. Three years after its introduction, the tax rate for those in the $500,000 to $1 million bracket fell by 31%, nearly five times the cut received by middle-income families earning between $30,000 and $40,000.[16]

The American social structure in the 1990s is defined by plummeting living standards for the vast majority of wage earners, large and growing income inequalities between employees and executives, and a small, extraordinarily wealthy, privileged, and nonproductive elite living on inheritance, speculation, interest, dividend payments, and other sources of unearned income rather than accumulating capital through long-term, large-scale investments. This dominant elite presides over an economy that cannot harness the great technological breakthroughs to increasing productivity and global competitiveness; it prefers to appropriate wealth through political and ideological power and inherited positions. This elite is to the nation's working class what the U.S. state is to the Third World: a powerful political/military and ideological force appropriating wealth at the cost of those below. The convergence of interests between the concentration of income in a parasitical class and the state's focus on military and ideological projections of power is no coincidence; they complement one another. Declining living standards and increasing wealth at the top is matched by large-scale transfers of income abroad for investment and consumption as the elite attempt to strengthen market shares.

DOWN AND OUT FROM CALIFORNIA TO THE NEW YORK ISLANDS

The extraordinary growth in the concentration of wealth and income in the United States since the late 1970s has been accompanied by rising levels of poverty, the decline of well-paid and stable jobs, increased exploitation of labor, a major contraction in the social wage, and a visible deterioration in the conditions of the American workplace.

Poverty within the working class is increasing. Between 1978 and 1988, the number of Americans living below the poverty line rose by 6 million to 32 million, or more than one in eight. During the Bush presidency, the numbers grew at an even faster rate: by 1992, another 6.2 million had slipped into this category.[17] But official figures alone do not convey the scope or severity of the problem: millions more were living in such tenuous circumstances (illness, job loss, divorce, etc.) that any single setback could have dire economic consequences.

According to a Census Bureau study, the proportion of full-time workers earning wages below the official federal poverty line for a family of four increased from 12% in 1979 to about 18% in 1990 (reaching as high as 25% in Mississippi).[18] The rise in the poverty rate for young families (headed by someone under thirty years of age) with children was equally dramatic: it doubled from 20% in 1973 to 40% in 1990; among young black families, the 1990 child poverty rate hit an astronomical 68%.[19] Between 1989 and 1992, the number of Americans depending on food stamps increased by almost 7 million to just under 27 million. This amounted to 10.4% of the population, the highest figure since the program's inception in 1964.[20]

If the 1980s was the period of greatest revival of U.S. global expansion, it was also a time of massive contraction of well-paid blue-collar *and* white-collar industrial jobs and even greater growth of low-paid jobs in the domestic sphere—a shift in employment patterns that accelerated the growth in poverty. Between 1979 and 1983, unemployment cut a swath through the white-collar sector: 3.8 million professional, managerial, technical, sales, and administrative support workers lost their jobs. But this figure paled in comparison with the job destruction that further decimated this sector during the 1987–91 period when a further 5.7 million white-collar workers received pink slips. Meanwhile, factory workers as a percentage of the total work force declined from 20% in the 1980s to 17% in 1991, and continues to fall.

This link between unemployment and poverty was sharply revealed in the devastating economic recession that hit the six New England states in 1990–91, the worst since the 1930s depression, that triggered massive job losses in virtually every economic sector including the highly paid white-collar workers. In the city of Nashua, for instance, high-tech and military industrial companies began laying off workers in the thousands—so much so that applications for emergency relief skyrocketed 72% between 1989 and 1990 alone.[22]

Instead of new manufacturing jobs, the 1980s witnessed a massive growth in service-sector employment: 21 million new jobs in retail trade and services, fast food restaurants, banks, hospitals, law firms, governments, and a large "contingent" work force of part-timers and temporaries. This sector, which now accounts for almost four out of every five workers, offers significantly lower wages and few, if any, social benefits. Employees in retail trade jobs, for instance, today earn less than 45% of the average weekly wage of the manufacturing worker. [23]

The trend toward part-time or temporary employment has sharply accelerated in recent years. According to federal government statistics, these accounted for about half of all new jobs in 1992, "up from less than a quarter of new jobs a decade ago." In the private sector, the figure was closer to two thirds. And of the 380,000 new jobs created in January 1993, no less than 90% offered only part-time work. [24] Such employment not only pays less but almost always lacks medical plans, pensions, and other social benefits. In their drive to capture world markets, the need to maximize profits demands that U.S. multinationals retain a core of managers and workers while temporarily employing and then discarding many more of the latter. The "globalization" of American capital is accompanied by the burgeoning growth of sweatshop labor: part-time workers earning poverty-level wages. If "proletarians" in the classical sense were laborers employed at insecure, low-wage jobs and lacking any bonds to the enterprise (pension plans, etc.) then, under the aegis of "international oriented capital," the late twentieth century is witnessing a large-scale re-proletarianization of the U.S. work force.

Paralleling the elite's focus on the areas of finance and overseas manufacturing has been a steady deterioration in conditions in the workplace for American wage earners. The U.S. occupational fatality rate is far higher than any other advanced industrialized country. American workers are thirty-six times more likely to be killed than Swedish workers and nine times more likely than their British counterparts. In the two-year period 1990–91, an estimated 20,000 deaths occurred in the workplace. Between 1973 and 1987, the number of workplace injuries increased by 12% and the severity of such cases by 32%. The AFL-CIO estimates that 6 million workers are injured yearly, 60,000 of whom are permanently disabled. The number of workdays lost due to on-the-job accidents has risen steadily over the past decade: between 1983 and 1987, the average for each

100 workers rose from 58.5 days to 69.9 days; from 1983 to 1990, the number of workdays lost to occupational injuries skyrocketed by 35%.[25] However, both government and independent monitors have voiced skepticism over the official death and injury figures, contending that "they may be underreported by as much as 50%."[26]

A particularly graphic example of the multitude of on-the-job dangers that workers are exposed to occurred in September 1991 when a fire at the Imperial Food products chicken-processing plant in Hamlet, North Carolina resulted in seventy-nine deaths or injuries. Most of those who died did so attempting to escape through six of the nine doors in the factory that were shut tight, "most padlocked by the owner to prevent employees from stealing his chickens."[27] The plant had never been inspected in its eleven years of operation. This was not surprising in a state with only sixteen Labor Department inspectors to deal with 160,000 employers. It often took the department as long as two years to respond to safety violations reported by workers. In 1990, the number of official inspections plummeted by over one-third compared to 1989, falling to the lowest level in sixteen years. While the number of state inspectors dropped by thirty-one during the decade of the 1980s, the number of employers increased by over 50,000.[28] The assistant labor commissioner, Charles Jeffress, observed that "the average workplace in North Carolina will be inspected once every seventy-five years."[29]

Nor have the depredations of the American workplace been confined just to adults. Since the early 1980s, there has been a remarkable growth in the use of child labor accompanied by a significant rise in the number of serious and fatal on-the-job accidents. Today, an estimated two million children aged fourteen to eighteen work excessive hours for virtual slave wages on farms, construction sites, or in the garment industry, fast food restaurants, mines, sawmills, and gas stations; and many of these jobs are extremely hazardous (e.g., operating powerful machines), resulting in amputations, burns, deep cuts, and electrocutions. Worse still, according to National Institute for Occupational Safety and Health investigators, several hundred illegal child workers are killed each year. And the vulnerability of these minors to catastrophic accidents is on the increase: the proportion employed in jobs the Department of Labor considers dangerous increased from 16% in 1991 to 25% in 1992.[30]

Despite clear evidence of rising workplace violations, an upsurge in sweatshops and the abuse of child labor laws, and what the National Safe Workplace Institute's Joseph Kinney called U.S. slippage "in its efforts to reduce job injuries,"[31] the Reagan administration weakened rather than strengthened safeguards and enforcement procedures. Between 1980 and 1985, the budget of the federal enforcement agency, the Occupational Safety and Health Administration (OSHA), was slashed to such an extent that almost one-third of its full-time employees were sacked. In 1992, the agency was operating on an annual budget just over half the appropriation for the Fish and Wildlife Service, employing only 1,200 inspectors who were responsible for monitoring 3.6 million work sites.[32]

Apart from government "deregulation" of the workplace, other factors, derived from the very nature of contemporary U.S. capitalism, have contributed to the worsening environment of American labor. One change that has greatly diminished existing safety programs has been the increasing role of speculation in the buying and selling of corporations, the explosion of leveraged buyouts. At the same time, technological changes to increase U.S. global competitiveness has placed greater emphasis on repetitive kinds of work, making employees more prone to severe ailments and other injuries. Between 1983 and 1987, for instance, repetitive trauma disorder cases soared from 26,700 to 72,940. Since then, the situation has reached epidemic proportions: more than 150,000 cases are now reported yearly, accounting for 56% of all workplace illnesses.[33]

Worsening conditions of employment have gone hand in hand with an intensified rate of labor exploitation. As salaries and wages have continued to lag behind inflation, workers have been forced to stay on the job longer hours to maintain existing living standards, with employers continually seeking to squeeze more out of their labor force in order to maintain profits in an increasingly competitive marketplace. For example, there have been numerous cases of New York City contractors passing the costs of low bids to win public works contracts onto their workers in the form of illegal wage cuts. Among those under investigation in 1992 was a contractor who underpaid more than 100 workers by $2.5 million by simply halving the prevailing hourly rate of pay.[34] Regarding wage levels and the length of the work day, the House Ways and Means Committee "Green Book," its annual study of social welfare statistics, points out that the incomes of the poorest 20% fell by 4.1% during the 1980s even though their number of hours worked increased by 4.6%.[35]

Between 1969 and 1987, the total annual working hours of full-time employees (88 million in 1989) jumped by 163; during approximately the same period (1973 to 1988), the amount of reported leisure time declined by more than one-third, from 26 hours to less than 17 hours a week.[36] While vacation time off for European workers increased during the 1980s, writes Juliet Schor, Americans' leisure time contracted significantly: "In the last decade, U.S. workers have gotten *less* paid time off—on the order of three-and-a-half fewer days each year of vacation time, holidays, sick pay, and other paid absences. This decline is even more striking in that it reverses thirty years of progress in terms of paid time."[37] What accounted for the increased hours worked was falling real wages and rising health care, housing, and household costs.

The shift toward global markets and production, external pressures from overseas competitors, the fear of layoffs and the proliferation of low-paid, non-unionized jobs with tightened management supervision and control, has led to a precipitous decline in the quality of life of American working people. It is also apparently contributing to the disintegration of families and the reemergence of the extended family. A 1989 University of Wisconsin study predicted that two-thirds (rather than the commonly assumed half) of all marriages would end in divorce and that adult children would rely more on their parents: "[the] drop in income caused by a change from an industrial to a service oriented society resulted in marriage no longer offering economic security to women and children."[38] Subsequent research (1992) began to discern a clear link between unemployment and the divorce rate, including a Census Bureau report which noted that "stresses arising from low income and poverty" appeared to play a major role in the breakup of two-parent families.[39]

The decreasing needs of an economy based on a thin strata of skilled employees and a mass of dead-end service jobs also coincided with the U.S. government's neglect of the public education system. The internationalization of capital finds its counterpart in the declining financial support for domestic education and the importation of academically trained labor. Between 1980 and 1988, inflation-adjusted education block grants to states were cut by 63%, vocational education funds by 29%, and college work study by 26.5%. Low-income, working-class families were especially disadvantaged: the number eligible to participate in the major federal education programs specifically targeting this group fell from 75% to 54%.[40]

The deterioration of U.S. education and its low priority in an economy dependent on high-tech industries and fictitious capital is evident in the low levels of student achievement. About 13% of American students leave school having failed to achieve a minimal reading skills level compared to only 4% in Europe and 1% in Japan. An analysis of 1980s high school graduates' test scores reveals that this was the first postwar generation that did not come to their first jobs better prepared than the preceding one. In fact, they were more than one year behind their 1966 counterparts.[41]

It is less costly for the U.S. to import qualified foreigners than to make investments to prepare local students for higher studies: in 1988, foreigners accounted for 46% of full-time graduate students in engineering and 26% in science as well as one-third of the 5,000 scientists working in the nation's Institutes of Health Research. Two years later, President Bush signed a measure tripling the quota intake of overseas skilled professionals from 55,000 to 140,000.[42]

The U.S. elite's dependence on private education, its failure, indeed refusal, to give priority to public education, and its preference for subsidizing mature students and trained professionals from abroad at the expense of the college-bound poor at home is indicative of its funding and resource priorities. The use of educated Third World Janissaries to compensate for the decay of internal educational structures reinforces American global power without affecting its corporate and military budget priorities.

GLOBAL POWER, THIRD WORLD HEALTH

Over the past decade or more, health conditions have worsened for Americans of every age: infants, adolescents, adults and the elderly. Reduced services, less public funding or increased costs have triggered all manner of negative consequences ranging from higher infant mortality rates, to the recurrence of nineteenth-century diseases, to more modern kinds of health epidemics. On most comparative indexes, the United States ranks last in health care but first in health costs among the world's industrialized countries.

Between 1960 and 1987, the U.S. slid from 12th to 22nd lowest in the number of infant mortality deaths per thousand of population while its emerging global economic competitor Japan, which began with a worse record, improved so much that it rose to first place.[43] Although UNICEF reported a slight improvement in the U.S. position from 22nd to 19th at the end of 1991, there was still little to be self-congratulatory about. In the District of Columbia, for instance, the rate was 23 in 1,000, more than double the national average. This meant that a baby born in the nation's capital was less likely to survive its first year than one born in Third World countries such as Cuba, Jamaica, or Malaysia.[44]

What largely accounts for America's woeful performance in this area is not, as some have suggested, crack and other drug-related factors; on the contrary, most deaths are due to illnesses (pneumonia, influenza) and infections that are easily preventable. Much more critical have been the federal budget cuts to health programs that helped make the 1980s a decade of "severe rollbacks in health insurance and available medical care."[45] The contraction in public health funds dramatically affected mothers' access to prenatal care, leading to a significant rise in the numbers of underweight babies. In 1991, the U.S. ranked 26th in the world behind such poor countries as Bulgaria in the percentage of low-birth-weight babies, affecting 6.9% of all children and 13% of black children. Nearly 40% of black women and almost one-quarter of all women receive no prenatal care in the first trimester.[46] And, according to a University of California study of more than 146,000 births during the years 1982 to 1986, where the parents lacked health insurance there was a 30% greater chance the babies would die, experience serious medical problems, or be underweight.[47]

In the United States, nearly 40,000 babies die each year before reaching their first birthday. Yet, an unpublished Bush administration interagency report conceded that 10,000 of these deaths could be prevented by the application of existing knowledge. With this kind of record, it is small wonder that the White House refused to sign an international treaty in 1991 which required, among other things, that nations guarantee the survival of children, as well as their protection and development.[48]

Studies by the Annie E. Casey Foundation, the Center for the Study of Social Policy, and Stanford University indicated that the social and health conditions of American children deteriorated through the 1980s across a range of indicators: percentage of low-birth-rate babies; violent death rate, ages 15–19; percentage of births to single teenagers; percentage of children in poverty; percentage of children in single-parent families; and levels of suicide, obesity, and behavioral disorders.[49] The suicide rate among teenagers, for example, jumped from 11.6 per 100,000 in 1970 to 11.9 in 1980 to 12.4 in 1988.[50]

The child poverty rate increased in 33 states during the 1980s. Overall, the number of children living below the poverty line rose by 1.1 million to 11.2 million or 18% of the nation's adolescents (20% for children under age six). Breaking down the figures by race revealed that only one in eight white children were affected compared with almost 40% of black children and over 32% of Hispanic children.[51] An estimated 40% of children also live in families that do not have employer-based health insurance. A Child Defense Fund survey found that the number of children covered by this kind of insurance actually declined 13.6% between 1977 and 1987[52]—in large part a consequence of the astronomical increase in low-paid, often part-time, nonunionized, service-sector employment.

In a withering indictment of the Reagan years, a congressional study published in late 1989 concluded that "a growing number of [the nation's] children . . . arrive at school ill-fed, in poor health and often homeless."[53] Under Bush, however, the problem actually worsened. Public health specialist Lucile Brown noted that 12% of children entering school in 1991 suffered from lead poisoning, malnutrition, prenatal exposure to drugs, low birth weight, and other problems hampering their capacity for learning.[54] But perhaps the 1992 Census Bureau figures said it all: the poverty rate for children under 18 had jumped to 21.9%, the highest figure in almost a decade.[55]

The health of America's teenagers has been no less plagued by physical and emotional problems, so much so that a joint national study by the Association of State Boards of Education and the American Medical Association in 1990 was forced to conclude: "Never before has one generation of American teenagers been less healthy, less cared for or less prepared for life than their parents were at the same age." Among its wealth of data, the study noted that 1 million (almost one in ten) teenage girls were becoming pregnant each year, 2.5 million adolescents were contracting a sexually transmitted disease, the teenage suicide rates had doubled since 1968, 10% of male and 20% of female adolescents had attempted to take their own lives, and that homicide was the leading cause of deaths among 15- to 19-year-old blacks.[56]

In an era of deregulation and financial profiteering, care for the elderly plunged to levels reminiscent of the early decades of the last century. At the end of the 1980s, more than 500,000 senior citizens in nursing homes and hospitals were being strapped to their beds and wheelchairs on a daily basis. One 84-year-old woman who was subjected to this form of unusual cruelty upon admission to a New York nursing home described the experience: "I felt tied up like a dog and I was so angry and ashamed. First I fought, then I cried, and then I just went into myself."[57] During 1989, according to federal surveys, about 41% of all nursing home residents were put in restraints compared with 25% in 1977.[58]

As if suffering from the indignities and depredations of a collapsing health care system was not enough, malnutrition among the elderly started to rise during the 1980s, often because of an inability to afford a balanced diet. The research director of the Tufts University Center on Hunger, Poverty and Nutrition Policy estimated that more than 3 million aged 65 or older experienced "chronic" hunger in 1990.[59]

The plight of the mentally ill also testified to the contrast between deteriorating social conditions and resurgent U.S. global power. In the words of a study prepared by the Public Citizen Health Research Group and the National Alliance for the Mentally Ill in 1990, "Not since the 1820s have so many mentally ill individuals lived untreated in public shelters, on the streets and in the jails." The study observed that there were more schizophrenics or individuals suffering from manic-depressive illness in prisons (100,000) than in mental hospitals (68,000).[60]

The cross-generational decline of health care has been matched by the reemergence of diseases presumed to have long since been more or less eradicated in the industrialized world. Years of large-scale budget cuts in public health programs have triggered a resurgence of virulent strains of tuberculosis in urban America. Between 1953 and 1985, the number of cases steadily declined from 84,300 to 22,000; in 1991, nearly 27,000 new cases were reported and the American Lung Association (ALA) predicts at least 50,000 new cases every year within a decade. Among children, the number of cases doubled in New York City and increased 40% nationwide during the latter half of the Bush presidency. The ALA's president commented scathingly, albeit indirectly, on the government's responsibility for this state of affairs: "Here we are in 1992 with cure rates lower than countries like Malawi and Nicaragua. We can't keep track of our patients, and all the evidence suggests more and more of them have TB that is resistant to our best drugs. We have turned a disease that was completely preventable and curable into one that is neither. We should be ashamed."[61] And, just as with the incidences of child poverty and low-birth-weight babies, the racial breakdown of the infection is symptomatic of the extent to which the process of internal decay is disproportionately affecting the non-white population: there were only 14.8 cases for every 1,000 New York City whites in 1990 compared to 62.1 for Asians, 71.4 for Hispanics, and 129 for black residents. This pattern was replicated nationwide.[62]

Health coverage for wage and salaried workers has declined significantly since the 1970s. During the last year of the Bush administration, the number of Americans without health insurance increased by 2.3 million to a record 38.9 million.[63] Then there are perhaps as many as 20 million individuals who have jobs that provide insufficient coverage in the event of serious illness. Blacks and Hispanics were far less likely to be covered than whites. According to Labor Department surveys, the percentage of fully paid health coverage for 31 million workers in large- and medium-sized companies (100 or more workers) fell from 75% in 1982 to 31% in 1989. Simultaneously, companies were passing more and more of the existing cost burden onto their labor force. During this seven-year period, the average monthly employee contribution to individual health care protection increased by a spectacular 178%.[64]

The erosion of health care coverage was partly a function of rising insurance costs that led many small businesses to terminate coverage for their employees. Between 1989 and 1990, 20% of companies offering insurance for workers' families abruptly dropped the benefit, forcing employees to pay an increasing percentage of their depressed earnings for skyrocketing medical costs.[65] But far more decisive were changes in the nature of American capitalism—the rise of the debt-merger mania-speculator environment—that contributed mightily to the more than 630,000 business bankruptcies during the 1980s that eliminated medical protection for millions of workers. This particular trend seems set to continue into the 1990s if the initial evidence is any guide: the combined number of individuals and businesses that filed for bankruptcy in 1991 increased by 21% over 1990 to a record 944,000 petitions.[66]

The rise in the number of uninsured workers was also a result of the millions of newly created part-time jobs during the 1980s.

Witness, for instance, the retail trade giants such as Sears, Roebuck (55% of all employees), K-mart corporation (45%), and the nation's largest retailer Wal-Mart (40%).[67] Only a very small proportion of these jobs offered any kind of health benefits.

Finally, the threat and reality of declining health coverage is not confined to America's working population; it extends to millions of retirees who are seeing promised comprehensive medical coverage benefits terminated or sharply reduced by former employers taking advantage of escape clauses giving them the right to change the benefits. During the 1980s, more than 2,000 companies discontinued their defined benefit pension plans and withdrew more than $21.5 billion in assets from the reserves earmarked for payments to hundreds of thousands of employees.[68] In mid-1992, David Walker, a former Assistant Secretary of Labor in the Bush administration, predicted that up to 95% of employers would eventually change existing employee benefit schemes.[69] Later that year, it was revealed that at least 23 large companies had terminated health benefits to thousands of retired employees. Meanwhile, dozens more announced there would be no coverage for future retirees and almost all other employers still providing benefits were busy implementing changes to reduce their share of the costs before January 1, 1993. After that date, a new rule obligated the owners of capital to subtract from profits the future costs of providing benefits to retired workers.[70]

Federal funding cuts to health care programs, eroding services, increasing costs and a dramatic fall in medical coverage for the work force, past and present, all testify to the persistent refusal of the U.S. state to deal with a critical socioeconomic problem that each year affects a larger number of the country's population.

DECAYING CITIES AND GROWING HOMELESSNESS

[B]ut I will tell you one thing, it is real hard to study, it is real hard to learn how to read, it is real hard to wash your clothes unless you have a place to live. It is just that simple. Housing is the foundation of it all.

Assisted housing resident in Los Angeles, 1992

A decade of state-authored deregulatory policies and budget cuts transformed almost every major American city into places of widespread poverty and homelessness surrounded by decaying physical infrastructure and other similar examples of urban blight. Between 1980 and 1990, direct federal aid to cities was slashed by close to 60%, from $47 billion to just under $20 billion.[71] The cities' share of federal government revenues dropped marginally from 19% in 1970 to 17.7% in 1980, and then plummeted to not much more than 6% in 1990.[72] "As a consequence [of these prolonged and massive cutbacks]," writes Demetrios Caraley, "the vast majority of large central cities of metropolitan areas were hurt; the disparities that already existed between rich and poor local and state jurisdictions got larger."[73] The cities were treated no more generously by Bush than Reagan. The proposed fiscal year 1993 funding for key urban programs amounted to only $13 billion.[74]

At a more general level, the steadily contracting federal investments in physical infrastructure (highways, mass transit, sewage plants, etc.) accelerated this process of urban decay. According to the House Public Works and Transportation Committee, an estimated 40% of the nation's bridges are in need of major repairs, not to mention the more than 28 million Americans who are served by inadequate sewage-treatment plants. Yet only 2.5% of all federal outlays in 1990 were earmarked for infrastructure investment—a 3% decline compared to 1965! In the last year of the Bush presidency, the U.S. was spending a miniscule 0.5% of its Gross Domestic Product on infrastructure, a quarter of what it allocated in the 1960s and far less than its major capitalist world competitors, Japan and Germany.[75]

The increase in the number of Americans living near or below the poverty level in the 1980s was concentrated in the central cities. The number of poor people living in the nation's major population centers increased by 5.7 million between 1970 and 1987 to 43% of the total.[76] The percentage of children living in poverty in the 100 largest cities was approximately 10% above the national average at the end of the decade.[77]

The deregulation of the banking industry under Reagan, which led to spectacular increases in real estate speculation and land and housing investments, had a catastrophic impact on the inner cities: hundreds of thousands were priced out of the housing market and became part of the long-term homeless population.

At the beginning of the Reagan presidency there were less than 250,000 homeless people in the United States, and perhaps as few as 100,000. Seven years later the number had jumped to around 600,000 and by the end of the Bush presidency nationwide research and surveys indicated that it may have surged to as many as two million annually.[78] The reasons for this dramatic increase was readily identifiable: the decline of affordable housing, the channelling of massive amounts of speculative capital into the real estate sector, low incomes and eroding welfare benefits, rising unemployment, and the failure of government payments to the poor to keep pace with inflation. Based on figures showing that rentals for less than $250 per month had declined by almost three million units between 1979 and 1987 while households receiving incomes of less than $10,000 annually had increased by a similar amount, a U.S. congressional report glumly observed that "the supply of affordable housing for low income households continues to decline."[79] A later study calculated that the "deficit" in rental units that the lowest 20% of income earners could afford doubled to 4.9 million between 1970 and 1990. Within the homeless category, families constitute the fastest growing component. In New York City, for instance, there were more homeless families in public shelters at the end of 1992 than ever before.[80]

U.S. government policy bears enormous responsibility for the worsening problem of homelessness not only due to its failure to regulate the activities of property/real estate speculators but also as a result of shifting spending priorities from subsidizing low-income public housing to subsidizing the corporate sector. In 1978, the Department of Housing and Urban Development's (HUD) budget for subsidized housing for the poor was approximately $31.5 billion; by 1988, it had dropped almost 75% to $7.8 billion. In 1980, Congress funded the construction of 50,000 public housing units;

federal budget cuts over the ensuing years reduced the number in 1992 to an estimated 4,000 units.[81] Furthermore, a 1992 congressional study found that HUD's annual $3 billion a year budget for building houses, razing slums, creating jobs, and providing other benefits to low- or moderate-income groups was in fact being invested partly in programs enriching private interests—in the form of low-cost interest loans to corporate giants like Sears, Roebuck, rich individuals including a Miami-based Saudi sheik, and a minor league New York hockey team.[82]

While the average number of weekly home foreclosures in cities across the nation during 1991 and 1992 reached levels not seen in decades, and public housing applicants in New York City could look forward to an estimated 18-year wait, low-income housing units were actually being demolished by the thousands in cities across the country and transformed into lucrative dwellings for the wealthy.[83] As a result, "more people [were] sleeping in city parks, under freeway viaducts, in abandoned cars and in saloon grade welfare hotels than ever before."[84] The diversion of funds to empire-building sectors (military, intelligence, etc.) and the conversion of millions of square feet of working-class areas and industrial sites into multi-million-dollar apartment buildings, as well as high-priced financial, tourist, and related service-type activities linked to the international economy, is merely the other side of the coin of rising homelessness in America.

THE "HIGHER IMMORALITY": CRIME AND DE-INDUSTRIALIZATION

In his classic 1950s study of America's power elite, C. Wright Mills described a small group of individuals pursuing their own self-interest at the expense of the public good. He termed their behavior a form of "higher immorality"—as distinguished from low-level kinds of criminal enterprise. Some three decades later, one could justifiably speak of the United States as going through an "era of higher immorality," so pervasive were the illegal and lawless activities of the major investment houses (Drexel-Burnham, Salomon Brothers, etc.), savings and loan institutions, and other financial sectors. Nor could this state of affairs have persisted without the involvement and complicity of senior Reagan administration officials, even reaching into the White House itself.

In many ways, though, the era of higher immorality label is more appropriate to describing the multitude of legal, routinized corporate decisions that produced a sustained shift of capital investment from industry to services, and from production in the local economy to the funding of overseas plants—to the accompaniment of an unparalleled deterioration in the domestic urban landscape. In the course of deindustrializing America's cities, whole households, social networks, and communities were systematically destroyed; families disintegrated and the crime rate soared. A study of five urban cities (New York, Detroit, Newark, Boston, and Philadelphia) over the period 1960 to 1986 revealed an inverse relationship between industrialization and crime: declining factory employment went hand in hand with spiralling crime rates.[85] Economic Policy Institute researchers confirmed this link after analyzing data gathered for thirty major metropolitan areas in the United States from 1976 to 1990. The study's key finding was that a 1 percentage point rise in the unemployment rate not only increased deaths due to heart disease (5.6%) and strokes (3.1%) but also those due to homicides (6.7%), violent crimes (3.4%), and property crimes (2.4%).[86] Furthermore, such episodes as the December 1990 U.S.-led military intervention in the Gulf showed that these twin phenomena were not unrelated to global empire building. While the Bush administration was aggressively mobilizing military and economic resources to "save" Kuwait and protect its petro-client monarchy in Saudi Arabia, domestic voices requesting an equivalent commitment by the White House to the problems of poverty and crime in America's cities went unheeded.

During the 1980s, the U.S. state channelled tens of billions of dollars into military spending, promoting corporate expansion, facilitating bailouts of savings and loan institutions and the conversion of capital to leveraged buyouts, and encouraging international financial and industrial investments. These decisions about resource allocation not only failed to generate expanding industrial employment and well-paid jobs (an antidote to the rising crime rate) but had a profoundly dislocating effect on the nation's working class. The only recourse left was to build more prisons. During eight years in office, New York's Governor Mario Cuomo presided over the most comprehensive prison construction program in the state's history including an additional 30,000 new beds. Nonetheless, running for a third term in 1990, he promised to make "criminal justice a top priority."[87] Nationwide, state prison construction budgets increased 73% between fiscal 1987 and fiscal 1991. In 1991, 44 states "were building new prisons or expanding existing ones."[88]

Neither additional prisons, more police, or proliferating anti-drug campaigns had any visible impact on the rising spiral of crime. The U.S. currently imprisons a larger share of its population than any other country. Notwithstanding the Reagan-Bush "harsher punishment" approach to dealing with crime, the number doubled between 1980 and 1990, reaching 1.1 million. The incarceration rate of 455 per 100,000 far exceeded the second ranking country, South Africa (311). The rate for black Americans was an extraordinary 3,370 per 100,000 compared to only 681 for blacks living in the global heartland of apartheid; there were five times more blacks (500,000) in U.S. jails than in South African jails. And even these stark figures do not adequately convey the extent of racial discrimination.[89] A study by the National Center on Institutions and Alternatives, for instance, found that in the District of Columbia, 42% of black males aged 18 to 35 were enmeshed in the criminal justice system on any given day in 1991—in prison (15%), on probation or parole (21%), and out on bond or being sought by police (6%).[90]

There was also an unparalleled increase in violent crime during the three decades to 1990. Over this period, the number grew by 355% on a per capita basis with only a marginal decline in the rate of increase during the Reagan-Bush era. According to the Sourcebook on Criminal Justice Statistics the rate jumped from 364 per 100,000 in 1970 to 597 in 1980 to 732 in 1990. Between 1989 and 1990, the number of homicides climbed by 9% to an all-time high of 23,440, the largest annual increase since 1979. This record lasted a mere 12 months: in 1991, 24,700 Americans were murdered.[91]

A principal contributor to the growth of crime in the 1980s was the "outward-looking" financial institution deeply involved in the laundering of narco profits. In 1984, the drug-dealing Bank of Commerce and Credit International (BCCI) transferred $37.5 billion worth of foreign currencies through a number of U.S. banks, including Bank of America, Security Pacific, American Express, Bank of New York, First Chicago, and its secretly owned First American Bankshares. In 1986, Bank of America was fined $4.75 million for money laundering. During the 1980s, the Medellin drug cartel laundered hundreds of millions of dollars via Bank of America, American Express, Citibank, Republic National Bank, Extebank, First American Bankshares, and other domestic financial institutions.[92] In 1989, bank investigators estimated "that as much as $100 billion from selling cocaine in the United States [was] being sent from the country annually through the electronic transfer of money from American banks to accounts in foreign countries. Furthermore, undercover federal agents who posed as money launderers and "discussed transactions" with these banks' executives did not find them "unwilling collaborators."[93] The Internal Revenue Service (IRS) ultimately prosecuted 55 American banks and between 300 and 400 officials, illustrative of the powerful economic links that bound speculator-finance capital at the top with the lumpen drug entrepreneurs during the Reagan presidency.[94]

Despite these successful prosecutions, the deregulatory climate and severe understaffing of those bodies charged with tackling the problem limited all efforts to make significant inroads into the bank-drug nexus. "Operation Greenback," the administration's main official force investigating money laundering (based in Florida) saw its staff of Customs, Drug Enforcement Agency, and IRS personnel cut from 71 in 1981 to 17 in 1989.[95] The chairman of the Senate

Subcommittee on Terrorism, Narcotics, and International Operations, John Kerry, was moved to declare that "control is so lackadaisi-
cal that it is almost damnable."[96] Since then, key anti-drug agencies
have continued to lose personnel. In September 1989, the Bush
administration launched a national drug control program; three years
later, the number of IRS drug and money laundering investigators
had actually declined.[97] Meanwhile, a $150 billion a year illegal
drug market in the United States[98] gives financial institutions at the
top and drug sellers at the bottom a major stake in continuing those
practices that feed into, and exacerbate, the socioeconomic decline
set in motion by the wholesale transfer of capital from local industry
to global financial and investment networks.

The connections between financial networks, narco dollars, and
the government's refusal to make available sufficient resources to
investigate the drug laundering industry have paralleled various manifestations of urban disintegration: the growth of a criminal class in
the United States controlling whole sectors of cities as well as parks
and public transportation sites; a reemergence of medical epidemics,
including a tenfold increase in crack-related emergencies between
1985 and 1987; and the appearance of a cohort of damaged children
born of drug-imbibing parents (900,000 in the three years to September 1992). Federal estimates place the cost to the state of subsidizing
economic-induced drug abuse at $60 billion annually.[99] However,
in a situation where the Latin American elites have over $250 billion
in assets invested abroad,[100] the U.S. overseas corporate-financial
class is quite willing to divert local resources to "drug abuse" in
order to maintain its ties to these foreign investors.

The U.S. domestic elite's response to urban decay and spiralling
crime rates has been to "bunker down" with the assistance of private
police forces, transport, schools, clubs, and the like. Some have
become virtually self-imposed prisoners in their million-dollar-plus
apartment houses: "Among the more affluent New Yorkers, there
is a tendency for them to cut themselves off from the city's public
places."[101] Others have simply fled the scene, opting for "the security
of the suburbs." Across the country, members of the class have "more

than ever isolated themselves from the rest of society." University of Chicago demographer Douglas Massey identified myriad signs of the elite's headlong drive into residential isolation,

> from the rise of thousands of "gated communities" to the proliferation of "shadow governments"—including the 150,000 homeowners' groups, community associations and other private entities that perform traditional public duties such as raising taxes and collecting garbage from those who can afford them.[102]

The growth of the international financial networks and the resurgence of U.S. global political and military power has been accompanied by rising economic and personal insecurity for the vast majority of America's urban dwellers: more real estate speculation, drug money laundering, deindustrialization, crime, prison spending; less social services, housing, well-paid manufacturing jobs. The ideology of "national security" used to justify global empire is one side of the coin; deteriorating cities and worsening life circumstances inside the empire is the other.

THE BIG SQUEEZE: UNEMPLOYMENT BENEFITS, FOOD PROGRAMS, PENSIONS

The 1980s was a decade of massive job losses that owed much to the policies of both the executive and legislative branches of government. Deregulation forced thousands of companies out of business, terminating hundreds of thousands of employees; major changes to the Internal Revenue Code did not extend to the provision allowing corporations a more or less unlimited writeoff of interest paid on borrowings which had devastating implications for workers because corporate debt "was being used increasingly to buy and then dismantle companies, not to build them"; amendments to the Bankruptcy Code enabled companies to declare insolvency and continue operating with greater ease than previously, resulting in the elimination of thousands of middle-income positions courtesy of a 155% rise in petitions filed in the 1980s compared with the 1970s.[103]

Unemployment at some time in 1991 affected one-fifth of the

total American work force.[104] In the New York region alone, the number of job losses between 1989 and 1991 erased 40% of the employment growth that occurred during the decade.[105] Official figures have consistently and substantially undercounted the actual numbers of unemployed in recent years, failing to take account of those so discouraged that they had given up looking; those forced into temporary, freelance, or part-time employment; and those working but barely surviving on the economic margins (low wages, few or no social benefits) who basically faced the same hardships and felt the same insecurities as those without any job at all. While the official rate stood 7.8% in June 1992 (or just under 8 million unemployed), the real rate was closer to 13% or more.[106]

In the 18 months since July 1990, 1.9 million jobs disappeared, including not just manufacturing-industrial positions but 525,000 retail trade jobs in the service sector. Of equal importance, this is not a cyclical phenomenon: it promises to be a long-term trend. In 1992, General Motors Corporation announced it would eliminate 74,000 jobs by 1995; six of the nation's largest companies (Exxon U.S.A., Hughes Aircraft, Aetna, Chevron, Digital Equipment, and Alcoa) sacked more than 23,000 workers; Amoco Oil Corporation disclosed that 15.7% of its 54,120 labor force would be laid off by the end of the year; in August 1992, 167,000 factory jobs disappeared as employment in this sector fell to its lowest level since April 1983; in December 1992, IBM said another 25,000 jobs would be terminated in 1993. An American Management Association survey of more than 800 companies found that one in four was planning to reduce its work force by mid-1993. Defense-related industrial positions that declined by 365,000 between 1987 and 1991 are projected to fall another 15% within four years. Among middle-level managers, the number of unemployed exceeded 600,000 in 1992. Dan Lacey of *Workplace Trends* predicted that the top 500 companies would fire at least 4 million workers.[107]

Between December 1992 and January 1993, while the number of unemployed Americans not even bothering to look for work jumped by over 500,000, the pace of corporate job dismissals accelerated. During the first weeks of 1993, Sears, Roebuck, Boeing, Pratt

& Whitney, McDonnell Douglas, United Technologies, Armco, and other major companies announced their intention to eliminate over 100,000 positions (combined)—mostly full-time jobs with health and pension benefits.[108] Corporate sackings in the New York region belied the "end of recession" media headlines: even the federal government acknowledged that the rate of decline in manufacturing jobs in this key sector of the domestic economy (270,000 or 24% of the total lost between 1987 and 1992) was showing no signs of slowing down.[109] Meanwhile, those still employed in the manufacturing sector today work more hours per week on average (over 41) than at any time in the last 26 years.[110]

The record reduction of interest rates by the Federal Reserve Board has manifestly not created new jobs. In a "post-industrial" economy it has, predictably, stimulated stock speculation to new heights. And speculators are betting on short-term profits based on the aggressive lay-off policies of the major corporations, rather than looking toward long-term investment in new production lines that would increase the work force, consumer confidence, and demand for goods and services down the line. Low interest rates do not stimulate investment in plant and equipment to create jobs in an economy with excessive productive capacity and debt. Corporations do not invest in expansion when they don't need it. Moreover, low interest rates and investment incentives typically quicken the growth of activities abroad; while the domestic economy wallows in deep recession, imperial capital grows. The convergence of speculative opportunities and international markets and investment sites reinforces the structural impediments toward reducing unemployment: long-term, large-scale unemployment appears to be the structural accompaniment of speculative capital at home and capital search for global profits.

While the government increases corporate tax reductions, allocates record amounts to bail out failing financial institutions, provides exceptionally generous subsidies for overseas investors and authorizes a military budget that is the highest in the world, the unemployed, the poor, and the elderly—those in greatest need of public assistance—are offered, at best, pittances and, at worst, nothing at all. Entering the 1990s, only 34% of jobless workers were deemed eligible to collect unemployment benefits, precisely because the official rate excludes the estimated 7.5 million involuntary part-timers and discouraged job seekers who have completely dropped out of the work force. Yet, the picture for the unemployed is even worse than these figures suggest: not only are average benefits, which are set by state governments, far below the poverty level; that minority of the real unemployed who fall within the official definition saw the duration of their benefits cut from 65 weeks to 26 weeks in 1991.[111]

The Reagan administration also savaged major federal welfare programs benefitting the poorest and neediest groups in American society. Aid to Families with Dependent Children (AFDC) and the food stamps program were slashed by 17.4% and 14.3% respectively. As a consequence, "at least 400,000 families lost their eligibility for welfare and nearly one million individuals lost eligibility for food stamps." Over seven times the number of black families were affected by the AFDC cuts than white families; in the case of food stamps, the ratio was just under three to one.[112] By 1988, the maximum AFDC payments in thirty-one states for a family of three was less than half the poverty level.[113] In the transition from Reagan to Bush, those seeking AFDC benefits and food stamps increased significantly while the amount and/or value of the funds provided continued their downward spiral. The number of families in the AFDC program grew by almost 1 million (or 24%) between mid-1989 and mid-1991. But the response of most state governments to this development mirrored federal policy toward those most in need: 40 legislatures voted to reduce benefits to this group for fiscal year 1992, producing the biggest annual decline in AFDC funding in over a decade.[114] Meanwhile, the House Ways and Means Committee released data showing that the purchasing power of (welfare and food stamp) benefits offered single mothers had fallen by an average of 27% in the two decades to the beginning of the 1990s.[115]

The government's food allotment program for poor women and children was another target of the Republican White House attacks on social sector spending. In May 1990, the New York Times reported major cuts to the program in half the states that included the elimination of thousands of poverty-stricken individuals from the program altogether. The Special Supplemental Food Program for Women, Infants, and Children (SSPW) supposedly covered 4.5 million expectant and new mothers and young children in dire poverty. But, by keeping the $2.1 billion allotment fixed while prices of basic food items increased, Washington forced the states to slash individual allotments. In Texas, for instance, one- and two-year-old infants had their cereal allowance cut by 33%; in California, with its booming global economy, local authorities cut the juice allowance for three- and five-year-olds, and abruptly terminated the cheese allocation to the detriment of "pregnant women, breast feeding women and infants whose diet has been diagnosed as inadequate but who show no clinical signs of malnutrition."[116]

The Bush priorities could not have been more starkly delineated: on the one hand, tens of billions of dollars appropriated to increase America's military capacity and finance the Gulf War; on the other, pursuing policies that cut back (directly or indirectly) funding for social programs designed to provide basic foods and other necessities for record numbers of children living in poverty and the rest of the domestic poor.

The cutbacks in domestic welfare programs have affected not only the young, the women, and the millions of unemployed, but also the nation's aging population. The increasing investments abroad during the 1980s were fueled partly by a substantial rise in the number of workers receiving no pensions or considerably reduced benefits. While the total labor force expanded by approximately one-fifth, the number of employees covered by government-insured pension plans fell from 49% in 1979 to 43% in 1991.[117] Central to any explanation of this trend is the shift from manufacturing to service-based employment: the substitution of low-wage, low-benefits work for well-renumerated, high-benefits positions. At the same time, large numbers of people reported their pensions shrinking, some to less than 20% of their retirement income. Inflation also continues to erode the value of those 75% of company payments that are not adjusted for cost-of-living increases.[118]

In the era of deregulation and corporate raiders, companies did more than just eliminate or reduce pension benefits. First, through substituting inferior plans for existing programs, they shifted more of the burden of financing onto their employees: corporate pension plan contributions fell from $54.4 billion in 1983 to $45.2 billion in 1988 as the owners gave priority to debt interest payments incurred as a result of massive borrowings.[119] Second, outright pillage of employee pension funds was a common feature of the 1980s as nearly 2,000 business owners removed $21 billion from these funds for use in unrelated areas.[120] Third, the Pension Benefit Guarantee Corporation (PBGC), the federal agency that insures corporate pension plans, saw its liabilities increase from $30 billion in 1989 to $51 billion in 1991—raising the specter of a major financial bailout in the near or medium future. And the PBGCs burden keeps getting heavier: the shortfall in the fifty companies with the largest underfinanced pension plans increased by almost $9 billion (to $38 billion) in 1992. This widening gap between corporations' guaranteed benefits and their lack of funds to meet employee retirement commitments simply further compounded the problems of a federal government whose own retirement program for civilian and military employees was underfunded by more than $1 trillion as Bush prepared to leave the White House.[121]

Nor have public-sector workers' pension funds been exempt from theft at the hands of their employers. During the two-year period 1990–91, at least seventeen cash-strapped state governments "cut or delayed contributions to their pension funds, seized money outright from pension accounts, or begun to debate similar measures." One of the more notorious cases involved a decision by California Governor Pete Wilson to take $1.6 billion from the coffers of the state's Public Employee Retirement System to cope with the problem of a $14 billion budget deficit as July 1991 and the start of the new fiscal year approached.[122]

Lastly, a particularly insidious example of robbing domestic wage earners to finance imperial politics has been the growth of Social Security payments and the uses to which they have been put. During the 1980s, this tax on all wage earners increased from 5.1% to

7.65%, or by almost 33%.[123] However, the government spent the surplus that accrued as if it were part of general revenues, thus masking the growing federal deficit. Without the exploitation of workers' financial surpluses, Washington would not have been able to cut the capital gains tax for corporations or fund its new military technology. Under the guise of financing social welfare, the Social Security tax therefore became, and remains, another tool for transferring labors' income into funding global expansion.

CRISIS IN THE SERVICE SECTOR

While American capital began the 1990s aggressively competing in the international arena, the single most powerful locomotive of new jobs in the 1980s—the service sector—started shedding hundreds of thousands of positions at both the top and lower ends, all in the name of "cost reductions." General Motors, Xerox, IBM, and other multinationals fired or prematurely retired middle managers, technicians and other white-collar employees with service-type responsibilities. Large numbers of white-collar workers in insurance, banking, and real estate were sacked during 1990 and 1991; in the debt-ridden financial sector alone, over 115,000 jobs were abolished.[124] Job losses in the transportation and telecommunications sectors added to this new class of unemployed professionals and managers.[125] Under the growing weight of deregulation, and profit and competitive pressures, the traditional corporate "social contract" of worker loyalty in return for secure employment disintegrated. Such devastation has been just as, if not more, widespread at the other end of the service industry: 525,000 retail jobs disappeared in the 18 months to December 1991.[126]

Whereas in the recession of 1981–82 there were almost no job losses among white-collar workers and the service sector was able to absorb a proportion of the discarded factory employees, in the "post-industrial" speculator economy this latter option no longer existed—except perhaps for marginal employment in the "informal sector." Moreover, debt-financed consumer spending that artificially stimulated the service economy in the 1980s was no longer operative:

the corporate raiders, real-estate speculators, leveraged buyouts, junk bonds, and the like had hollowed out the industrial base of the nation's economy. The outcome has been a pattern typical of capitalist development: the concentration and centralization of capital ("the strong getting stronger") in those service sectors such as retail trade and banking. Its accompaniment was the reproduction of a classic feature of industrial capitalist society. "Companies are working overtime to increase efficiency," wrote a correspondent for the *New York Times* in early 1991, "trying to squeeze more sales out of the existing work force or maintain sales with a smaller staff."[127]

As the service economy sank into crisis, amid growing concentration of corporate economic power at the top, the absence of a dynamic industrial sector vitiated the possibility of absorbing displaced workers. And because the financial sector and government were burdened by huge debt and rising deficits, neither were in any position to lend and spend the service economy out of its current predicament. The latter's precariousness was evident in precisely that area to which most American corporations have devoted their greatest attention: the global economy. The surplus in U.S. trade in services and investment peaked at $43.8 billion in 1981 and then plunged to only $15.3 billion in 1988. However, the 1988 figure would have been even lower had not the Department of Commerce redefined education, travel, and other categories as services. In the absence of these changes, department officials claimed that the $15.3 billion "surplus" would have been transformed into a $176 billion deficit.[128]

While particular sectors of the service economy remained competitive in world markets (accounting, medical services, computer services, insurance, etc.), the investment account continued to demonstrate the global weakness of the American economy during the Reagan/Bush years: receipts from U.S. assets abroad were increasing at a slower rate than income payments on foreign assets in the imperial center. Sustaining global military and ideological power, and fueling speculative activity at home combined to undermine the "post-industrial" economy, in the process weakening the very economy that the service sector exists to service.

DISINTEGRATING CIVIL SOCIETY:
THE COLLAPSE OF ORGANIZED LABOR

Historically, the theory of democratic politics was based on a strong civil society resting on a powerful set of autonomous organizations linking citizens to political institutions. For wage and salaried workers, trade unions were recognized as one of the most important vehicles through which they could express their socioeconomic interests and influence state policy.

In the era of ascending imperial power, coinciding with the end of World War II, unions represented over 35% of American labor and were able to extract social benefits and improve living standards in return for supporting Washington's policy of global expansion. The AFL-CIO leadership was an active supporter of the Cold War and U.S. military intervention throughout the Third World which served to strengthen the military-ideological instrumentalities of the imperial state at the expense of the economic-industrial; in Latin America, it sided with U.S. client regimes, even participating in military coups that brought to power anti-working-class governments who, in turn, replaced militant unions with pliant ones led by AFL-CIO-trained functionaries willing to maintain "discipline" and keep wages low—in order to attract large-scale inflows of U.S. corporate capital.[129] At home, meanwhile, it was not unusual for the biggest multinationals to agree to union demands for generous wage and fringe benefits: monopoly profits abroad, the dominance of world markets, and high levels of unionization in key industrial sectors (automobiles, steel, electrical, machine tool) ensured a "trickle down" effect from overseas and domestic expansion.

Today, however, union membership is at an all-time low. During the "labor bashing" Reagan years, the slide quickened noticeably: from 35.5% in 1945 to 23% in 1980 to 16.8% in 1988. This downward trend persisted under Bush. Within the private sector, organized labor has been even more thoroughly decimated. From a peak membership of 35.7% in 1953, it dropped to approximately 17% in the mid-1980s, currently stands at 12%, and continues to fall.[130] Paralleling these membership losses over the past decade or so, unions have become transmission belts for reduced wages, social benefits, and living standards dictated by the state and the corporations. The union leadership has, in effect, abnegated its traditional responsibilities to its constituency. Indicative of the "new compliance" has been a steep decline in the number of strikes involving 1,000 or more workers from an annual average of at least 300 during the 1960s to just over 150 in 1980 to a mere 40 in 1991.[131]

While the White House projects U.S. power abroad, organized labor has been forced to confront the long-term, devastating consequences that unconditional support for global interventionism has had on its ever-shrinking membership. The majority of organized workers are no longer in the manufacturing-industrial sector; they have been replaced by public employees, and food and service workers.[132] Industries such as steel, coal, and automobiles that were once almost totally unionized have experienced a sharp increase in non-union labor. Over the past decade, the labor bureaucracy has acquiesced to capital's efforts to shift more of the burden of health and other social benefits onto the wage and salaried earners and offered little resistance to the revival of the minimum-wage, unorganized sweatshops on a large scale, especially in the garment industry, and the growing exploitation of child labor. Perhaps the AFL-CIO's greatest failure, though, has been its incapacity to organize the fastest growing and poorest paid sector of American labor: in 1990, only 6% of workers in private-sector service jobs were unionized.[133]

When the Reagan administration declared virtual "open war" on what remained of the labor movement in 1981 by firing 11,500 air traffic controllers and destroying their union, it signalled the beginnings of an increased resort to strike-breaking and worker "lockouts" by the owners of capital. Unions unwilling to capitulate to state-corporate demands in a period of deepening recession could expect to suffer part, or all, of the same fate that befell the air traffic controllers (e.g., Eastern Airlines and Greyhound Bus workers). Since Reagan left the White House, this anti-labor offensive has shown no signs of abating. In April 1992, the union movement experienced its worst defeat since 1981 when the United Auto Workers (whose own membership declined by approximately 600,000 during the 1980s) called off a five-month strike by employees of Caterpillar Inc. over management decisions to cut wages, and health and retirement benefits. Under the threat of mass firings, the union directed their members to return to work, accepting company terms it had rejected three months earlier. Caterpillar issued its ultimatum while acknowledging that its employees were more productive than any of its global competitors. But, as Jeff Faux, president of the Washington-based Economic Policy Institute commented: "Cat wants high productivity and low wages. The net result is to erode living standards."[134]

Despite the highly successful state-corporate offensive against organized labor, the union leadership itself cannot be absolved of all responsibility for its current plight: its incapacity to defend members' interests in collective bargaining; its unwillingness or inability to challenge long-standing commitments to Washington's global politics; and the increasing transformation of unions into business promotional "social service organizations" providing credit cards and insurance schemes at the expense of aggressively seeking to expand membership and act as a representative of traditional working-class interests.[135] Particularly striking has been the decline in union representation elections from 7,000 to 8,000 in the 1970s to half that number during the 1980s. "Even before this dramatic drop-off," writes David Moberg, "estimates are that a third of the decline in union organizing success resulted from decreased union organizing activity," Yet, while workers left unions in record numbers in the 1980s "overall union dues income rose in real terms."[136]

As U.S. global capital expands to border industries in Mexico, introduces high-tech computers, and intensifies pressures at the workplace, the stable, full-time labor force shrinks apace, safety conditions deteriorate, and living standards fall. Corporations no longer view unions as "partners in global expansion" precisely because in the 1990s they do not need to: trade unions are so powerless that there is no necessity to share global profits; in a world of international markets, labor is seen as a cost, not a consumer. In this era of global expansion, the state is similarly dismissive: preoccupied with bolstering capital's competitive position abroad, it moves to erode the union movement's bargaining position at home.

The erosion of trade union power has been, in large part, a consequence of the policies pursued by the labor bureaucracy that have been instrumental in facilitating U.S. global expansion. The latter would almost certainly not have taken the form it has if there existed an American labor movement representing a substantial proportion of the work force and intent on securing improved living standards for its members, influencing state policy toward industrial development instead of military-ideological "overreach," and opposing intervention in the Third World to create low-wage havens for multinational capital. In other words, the demise of trade unionism in the United States has been a necessary accompaniment to the rise of the imperial state.

POLITICAL DECAY: MASS ABSTENTIONISM AND THE FINANCIAL CONTROL OF ELECTIONS

There is deep unease within the elite: the political system has become so emptied out that the claims of the political leadership to speak in the name of the people or nation increasingly ring hollow. Just over one-third of the voting-age population cast their ballots in the 1986 and 1990 congressional elections. Only 55% were sufficiently motivated to do likewise in the 1992 presidential election, a slight rise over the barely 50% who participated in the 1988 contest for the White House.[137] According to E.J. Dionne in his study *Why Americans Hate Politics*, the reason for the 1988 presidential turnout (the lowest in over 60 years) was obvious: "most of the issues Americans really cared about had gone largely undiscussed [by Bush and Dukakis]."[138] Even those who continue to participate in the political process often do so with a sense of extreme pessimism. "You get so disgusted with them, you don't feel like you have a choice," remarked an eligible voter. "If you do vote, you feel like you're voting for the lesser of two evils."[139] In recent years, the phenomenon of non-voting has spawned a plethora of studies by academics, foundations, and research institutes based on the belief that American democracy is not working in the way these authors desire it to.

One of the crass practitioners responsible for subordinating politics to the financial power of the rich—Lee Atwater, former chairman of the Republican Party—cynically summed up the reasons for popular abstention:

> If you want to look at a solid trend for the last 15 or 20 years it is that the American people are cynical and turned off about all the institutions and politics is one. . . . Bull permeates everything. . . . the American people think politics and politicians are full of baloney. . . . They think the media and journalists are full of baloney. They think big business is full of baloney. They think big labor is full of baloney. To single out politics is making a grave mistake. [140]

The financial power of corporate America gives it a dominant role in shaping and influencing the political process. Between 1970 and 1988, money spent on all advertising during election years increased from less than $50 million to over $225 million; in 1990, close to half a billion dollars was spent on races for the House of Representatives and the Senate; in 1992, this figure skyrocketed to a record $678 million. [141] Corporate funding of elections, especially through the mass media, has enabled this elite sector to assume control over electoral agendas, de facto expropriating the voting population of any influence over issues, candidates, or parties. And, in recent years, corporations and wealthy individuals have increasingly exploited a legal loophole in congressional restrictions on large donations to electoral campaigns by giving to political parties instead of directly to candidates. During the 1988 presidential contest, Bush and Dukakis fundraisers each benefitted to the tune of $25 million of this so-called soft money; in 1989–90, the Democratic and Republican national party committees raised an additional $25 million in soft money while a further $18 million went to nine state party committees; in the 1991–92 electoral cycle, this figure soared to around $70 million, of which more than 90% came from corporations (particularly those in such heavily regulated sectors as securities and investment, oil and gas, insurance, tobacco, and real estate) and rich individuals. [142]

Among the heaviest donors are those seeking or dependent on government favors to maximize profits. The agribusiness giant and the nation's largest producer of ethanol, Archer Daniels Midland Corporation, gave more than $1 million in soft money contributions to the 1992 Republican presidential campaign. A major beneficiary of state subsidies, pricing supports, and associated tax breaks, Archer Daniels received exceedingly generous treatment from the Bush administration during the election year. This included an announcement of $350 million in new tax subsidies for Ethanol and new federal regulations that would require gasoline sold in five U.S. cities to be blended with ethanol to comply with Clean Air Act standards. Atlantic Richfield Company (ARCO), another major soft money donor to the Republican Party (over $515 million for the Bush reelection effort), was also "rewarded" for its support. During the 1990 debate on amending the Clean Air Act, for instance, the White House completely reversed its position and endorsed "a measure that ARCO was pushing hard to allow the use of 'reformulated gasoline' instead of cleaner alternative fuels."[143]

But even these sizeable donations are dwarfed by the funds lavished on the political class by the real estate industry. During 1989 to 1991, their political action committees (PACs) contributed more than $11.2 million to the Democratic and Republican party organizations and key members of Congress. This was topped up in 1989–90 by another $5.2 million given to party organizations and their congressional candidates by individuals in firms linked to the industry. Only a matter of weeks after a private meeting with top real estate executives and lobbyists, President Bush proposed a number of lucrative tax breaks for industry developers in his January 1992 State of the Union address. Congressional democrats added to the distinct impression that the investment "payoff" was imminent. They "not only embraced Bush's proposals, they expanded them, raising the likelihood that new incentives worth billions of dollars to real estate interests will be a central element of any tax legislation this year."[144]

The "baloney" referred to by Lee Atwater is recognition by the electorate that whatever the candidates and campaigns promise, they will not influence the major political decisions: the political class will pursue the political agenda of its paymasters, the corporate, banking, and property-owning elites. The electorate's cynicism reflects a clear understanding of the double discourse that permeates American politics: the politicians talk to the people and work for the rich. Or as one voter put it: "They don't really care about people. They take care of their friends, the people who give them money."[145] The profound structural reality about the political system is that both parties compete for financing among the rich, pursue the neoliberal agenda, and are unconditionally committed to the international strategy of the dominant elites including the diversion of resources from the domestic economy.

A political class beholden to multi-million-dollar campaign funders cannot articulate issues that engage the majority, thus the emphasis on trivia, vacuous campaign slogans, personalities, and the rest of the criticisms familiar to most Americans. By alienating the majority of low-income voters and assuring their abstention, the corporate and banking elites are free to influence and manipulate the minority that does vote by imposing constraints on the candidates and programs that are contested.[146] Moreover, the concentration of power in non-elected executive officials further enhances the state-economic elite relationship. The net result is a highly elitist political system, representative of a narrow class and devoid of popular content, either in the choice of political leaders, influence over policy debates, or political benefits. The electoral process is increasingly a noisy distraction, the public is an alienated and impotent victim, and the elite have the most accessible, representative, and responsive regime imaginable. The decay of the domestic political system—a disenfranchised electorate and non-representative political leaders—is both cause and consequence of the robust U.S. global ascendancy. Disarticulation of political movements is a necessary precondition for reallocating income upward and outward. And the growth and concentration of power in global executive elites brings as its consequence the impoverishment of domestic forms of political representation.

The 1980s witnessed the consolidation of a new political system:

(1) elite executive power, coherent with the international capital elites and the global military-ideological apparatuses of the state; (2) an impotent, occasionally testy, professional political class in the Congress that investigates excesses, but ultimately conforms to the global elite-executive strategies and alliances; as a group, it is submissive to those above and increasingly dissociated from the populace below; and (3) at the bottom, a fragmented mass competing over scarce resources, divided by sectoral interests, alienated from the political class, isolated from the ossified and declining trade union bureaucracies, with neither a political perspective nor a capacity to generate a national political movement to challenge the layers of political structures blocking new initiatives.

The alienation of voters with the elite-dominated, globally oriented political system entering the 1990s was strongest among younger voters (39% of non-voters) and those reporting incomes under $30,000 (53%). Civic impotency was generalized among voters and non-voters: 54% of the former and 62% of the latter admitted that "people like themselves do not have much say about what government does"; and three-quarters of both groups "trust[ed] government to do what is right only some of the time or never."[147] These sentiments of the effectively disenfranchised extended to both political parties and beyond to the elite globally oriented policies and structures of the political system.

While surveys regularly showed a large majority of Americans demanding greater federal government action to improve the education system, make health care less expensive and more accessible, clean up the environment, and tackle the crime problem more effectively (provide "safe streets"), polls taken during 1991 and 1992 revealed that anywhere from 60% to over 80% of eligible voters had little or no confidence in the ability of elected officials to solve these most pressing of problems. In a March 1992 poll conducted by the American Viewpoint Survey, almost three-quarters of the respondents agreed with the statement that "the entire political system is broken. It is run by insiders who do not listen to working people and are incapable of solving our problems."[148] A *Washington Post-ABC News* poll completed in early July 1992 found the level of disaffection at an all-time high: 82% of respondents agreed that both Democratic and Republican Parties "are pretty much out of touch" with popular needs and concerns.[149]

Overseas military interventions serve to extend the domains of global hegemony and to distract the mass from the worsening domestic conditions caused by the diversion of resources to further imperial needs. Bathed in chauvinist froth, the public submitted to another round of social budget cutbacks while living standards continued to erode and personal insecurity increased even as it told pollsters that the Bush administration "shouldn't think so much in international terms but concentrate more on our own national problems."[150] Voting without confidence in the politicians, expectations of any influence becomes an empty ritual; symbolic gratification from global military victories distract from visible socioeconomic deterioration at home. But this has allowed the policymakers to pursue their global political-economic agendas unhindered by internal opposition. The degradation of democratic politics—its hollowed-out character, widespread popular distrust and impotence—are the outcomes of the imperial presidency and the optimal conditions for projections of global power.

CONCLUSION

In the previous chapter we argued that, within a context of increasingly sharp competition and declining power in specific economic spheres, the U.S. still remains the preeminent actor in the global system. In this chapter we have demonstrated that the fact of U.S. global power is intimately linked to economic decay and social deterioration at home. This poses the question of why the U.S. cannot bolster its political and economic position abroad and, at the same time, address the needs of the national economy?

Today, American global power is largely based on state subsidies, promotion, and financing (or intimidation). As the U.S. overseas capacity grows amid rising competition, a zero-sum game emerges: what is spent or invested abroad is largely at the expense of the domestic economy. Moreover, the allocation of state revenues and private earnings between the domestic and overseas social forces is largely shaped by the balance of power between them. Since the 1970s, there has been a decisive shift in political power toward the export and global elites at the expense of wage/salaried and domestic-oriented forces; representatives of global interest penetrate all levels of executive and legislative power. The structural links between "global empire builders" and the state is far more extensive and profound than what is commonly described as the "military-industrial complex." A growing proportion of profits of the largest corporations are earned in the world market; local producers are seen increasingly as a cost not as consumers. The problem for the empire builders is how to reduce local costs (pensions, employment benefits, etc.) to ensure profits in international markets.

The overseas investors do not need a large, healthy, and educated work force to reproduce capital. Their needs are for an elite, specialized, skilled labor force—to provide financial services and staff-automated factories. Hence the deterioration of health, skills, and education does not greatly affect the export elites. Payments for social services are seen as a cost not as a potential benefit. So what is "bad for the country" or the "national economy" is not necessarily so for America's global actors.

Finally, U.S. global power needs to appropriate local resources because of the decline of U.S. competitiveness in the world market of the 1990s. In an earlier period, immediately after World War II, the U.S. as the sole capitalist economic superpower was able to dominate trade and investment markets, extract monopoly profits, and thus finance expansion from its overseas profits as well as domestic social programs and wage increases. With the entry of new global competitors, U.S. corporate profits are under pressure and their capacity to extract above-average profit rates has declined. The large-scale, long-term financing to sustain international competitiveness more and more revolves around appropriating national resources, as well as intensifying the exploitation of traditional areas of hegemony (Latin America and Canada) through free-trade agreements. In the sphere of global political-military power, parallel developments have taken place. Previously, the dominant position of the U.S. economy in the global sphere was instrumental in financing the state's global military-ideological apparatus. With the decline of global profits, the state has been forced to divert resources from the domestic economy (especially its social programs) to sustain global military, ideological, and economic expansion.

EPILOGUE

THE CLINTON ADMINISTRATION: GLOBAL LEADERSHIP VS. DOMESTIC RECOVERY

In April 1993, President Clinton met with Boris Yeltsin in Vancouver to discuss U.S. aid to the disintegrating Russian economy. What was at stake we were told was the salvation of the Yeltsin regime and its efforts to convert Russia to a capitalist economy. Clinton posed the issue in terms of a historical opportunity to consolidate the power of pro-Western rulers and accelerate the privatization process. The symbolism projected by the summit was profound: the leader of a former superpower rapping the beggars cup (like some Third World supplicant), beholden to the largesse of its historic adversary. But, if this watershed meeting reaffirmed the decline of Russia as a global actor it also revealed that Washington's new ascendancy—its position as the sole superpower—was more symbolic than fact.

Clinton's announcement of a $1.6 billion package of credits and grants offered little basis for pulling the Russian economy out of its tailspin, and thereby sustaining the Yeltsin regime. At the same time, the White House launched a $4 billion multilateral fund to promote privatization in Russia but was only prepared to contribute $500 million of this total, the rest to come from the G–7 nations, the International Monetary Fund, the World Bank, and other international institutions.[1] The message could not have been telegraphed more clearly: despite its superpower status, the U.S. is no longer capable of financing the consolidation of a new and important sphere of influence.

Further preventing the Clinton administration from pushing a multi-billion aid program to finance the "opening up" of Russia to U.S. extractive and industrial multinationals and financial institutions was the economic decay and social polarization that had become so much a feature of American society under Reagan and Bush, and was instrumental in the electorate's turn to the Democrats in November 1992. The decline in living standards over the past twenty years may have helped the American public realize the conflict between "empire" and "republic." Corporate flight to low-wage countries and social-sector cutbacks that accompanied massive increases in military spending during the Reagan-Bush era to fund intervention abroad may have heightened popular perceptions that the domestic economy was being pillaged to sustain "global leadership." Certainly, public opinion polls throughout the 1980s and early 1990s consistently demonstrated that overwhelming majorities of Americans are opposed to imperial politics, whether it takes the form of military intervention in Central America, large-scale subsidies to American investors abroad, or massive aid programs to bolster the economies of new client states.

The fundamental choice facing the Clinton administration was whether to follow the Bush policy of global empire building or to reconstruct the nation's economy and society. The choice was and is Empire or Republic? It is nonsense to talk of maintaining global leadership and rebuilding America. Simply put, there are not enough resources to do both. The correlation is straightforward: as the empire grows, the domestic economy weakens. Deteriorating cities and Los Angeles-type riots are the price of Desert Storms. Declining manufacturing investments in the U.S. are the counterpoints to large-scale investments overseas. The cleavage between the empire-oriented elite and the American public widens.

CHANGING NATIONAL ECONOMIC PRIORITIES?

During his election campaign, President Clinton implicitly recognized that empire building abroad and the reconstruction of the domestic economy were incompatible. So too did a clear majority of voters who preferred the Clinton emphasis on "rebuilding America" in contrast to Bush's preoccupation with "global leadership." Armed with an impressive mandate, Clinton entered the White House publicly declaring his intention to focus on the home front while accepting U.S. global commitments in Central Europe, the Middle East, southern Africa, and elsewhere. Furthermore, he acknowledged that the most critical problems facing the U.S. economy were "longer-term and structural."[2]

On taking office, however, he immediately proceeded to move in the opposite direction: revitalizing urban America took a back seat to bailing out Yeltsin; a critical view of the North American Free Trade Agreement (NAFTA) gave way to an emphasis on expanding and fast-tracking the program; instead of significant cuts in military and intelligence spending programs, the projected Clinton defense budgets for 1994 through 1998 indicated far more limited savings while administration officials expressed their opposition to any major tampering with the spy budget. This shift reflected the institutional power of those economic forces who brought Clinton to power and are disproportionately represented in the highest echelons of his government. Clinton is a new breed of Wall Street populist, one who talks to the people but works for the internationally oriented corporate elite.

There was perhaps no more striking illustration of Clinton's reversal of election priorities than his allocation of key economic and foreign policy positions to individuals who were oriented toward "global leadership": free traders and promoters of the multinational investment and banking community, and advocates of projecting American power abroad, including intervention in the Third World.

Asked to comment on the new administration's economic program, William Kristol, chief of staff of former Vice-President Dan Quayle, perceptively observed: "What is striking [about the program] is that there is this class warfare rhetoric, but what's creepy is how cynical it is. . . . He doesn't believe in this rhetoric. He has a cabinet full of millionaires."[3] Almost 80% to be precise (a figure higher than for the Reagan and Bush cabinets), most of whom accumulated their wealth during the speculator ("making money, not goods") decade of the 1980s. While the cabinet partially mirrored the nation's gender and racial diversity, it clearly did not reflect the class differences in the economic system. The president's senior economic advisor is, coincidentally, the richest member of his administration. Robert Rubin cochaired one of the world's most powerful brokerage-investment firms, Goldman Sachs & Co., and in 1992 alone received $26.5 million from the partnership that was augmented by millions more from investments in real estate, oil, and gas, and other partnerships. In a letter to former private clients after accepting the White House offer, Rubin indicated that his skills and influence would not be lost to the corporate world: "I also look forward to continuing to work with you in my new capacity."[4]

The new treasury secretary, Lloyd Bentsen, formerly chairman of the Senate Finance Committee, possessed assets worth almost $6 million, owned substantial real estate holdings, graced the boards of a number of banks and insurance companies, and had long been dubbed "loophole Lloyd" for his aggressive support of corporate tax breaks, especially for oil and gas interests and real estate developers. The response of corporate America to Bentsen's appointment was enthusiastic, to say the least. Charles DeBona, president of the American Petroleum Institute, was positively ecstatic: "Our only wish is that he could be cloned, and I think most business would feel that way, not just the oil industry."[5] The appointment of Roger Altman to be Bentsen's deputy was additional testimony to Clinton's embrace of Wall Street. As a senior treasury official during the Carter presidency, Altman played an active role in facilitating the Chrysler bailout. During the 1980s, he was vice-chairman of The Blackstone Group, an investment banking firm that accumulated huge profits through participation in the flood of mergers and acquisitions, and leveraged buyouts that characterized those years.

Millionaires were also placed in charge of the Departments of Labor (Robert Reich) and Commerce (Ronald Brown), and U.S. trade policy (Mickey Kantor). Brown was a lobbyist for a number of Japanese multinationals, the Duvalier family in Haiti, and the American Express Company, and continued to receive a salary from his law firm Patton, Boggs and Blow after being elected chairman of the Democratic National Committee in 1989. Kantor was a partner in the Washington law firm of Mannatt, Phelps, Phillips and Kantor which also had a number of prominent Japanese clients.

Some of Clinton's most influential foreign policy appointees had similarly powerful links to corporate America (and its multinational sector). Secretary of State Warren Christopher, whose personal worth exceeded $4 million, was the chair of one of Los Angeles' premier law firms, O'Melveny & Myers, that represented a number of U.S. and Japanese corporate giants; Deputy National Security Council advisor Samuel Berger directed the international trade group of the powerhouse Washington law firm Hogan & Hartson, and acted as a lobbyist for Japan's Toyota corporation; while James Woolsey, the president's choice to head the CIA, was a prominent Washington lawyer (Shea and Gardner) who happened to be a director of the Martin Marietta corporation, producers of the MX missile, and specialized in representing major defense contractors—most recently, McDonnell Douglas and General Dynamics in a suit against the U.S. government for cancelling purchases of the A-12 airplane.

Just as Clinton's personnel appointments ran counter to his campaign rhetoric about "rebuilding America," so too did the policies pursued during his first year in office—that conformed more to the structures of U.S. power linked to empire building (and domestic decay) than to the requirements of the national economy.

The apparent contradiction between the economic and class linkages of those appointed to the most senior positions within the Clinton administration and the new president's populist image and rhetoric can be resolved by briefly examining key features of the government's economic program during its first year in office—in order to identify who paid and who benefitted.

In February 1993, having campaigned on an explicit promise to reduce taxes on the middle class, Clinton submitted the outlines of his proposed fiscal year 1994 budget to Congress that included a regressive energy tax and higher taxes on social security benefits affecting both the middle and working classes. The top personal income tax was to rise from 31% to 36% with the expectation that this would bring in an extra $126 billion over the next four years. However, such an estimate seemed wildly inflated given the capacity of the rich and their tax lawyers and accountants to find loopholes in any program.

Instead of paying additional taxes, the top income earners could choose to defer monies, put it in tax shelters, channel it into areas not subject to federal tax (e.g., municipal bonds), or seek to change ordinary income into capital gains where the top tax rate promised to be significantly lower.[6] In any event, this proposed increase was but a fraction of the rate at which the very rich were taxed between 1964 and 1980 (70%) and still well below the figure for the first six years of the Reagan presidency (50%). The sum total of Clinton's "increase" was likely to do little more than perpetuate the tax inequities of the late Reagan and Bush presidencies.

Nor would the decision to increase the top corporate tax rate by 2% have any real negative consequences for big business and real estate interests as it promised to be more than matched by new tax credits and other concessions over the next four years. Already, the new administration had decided to partially restore a generous tax break eliminated during a major overhaul of the federal tax code in 1986 (over the opposition of then Senate Finance Committee chairman Lloyd Bentsen) that allowed real estate owners to claim deductions for losses on real estate investments to offset income from other businesses. Clinton also proposed making it easier for pension funds to invest in real estate ventures.[7]

In the budget package eventually submitted to Congress, the administration included a major concession to those earning over $100,000 who would be paying 90% of the proposed tax increases: they could spread their 1993 payments over two years. "In effect," wrote John Cushman in the *New York Times*, "they will be getting a two year loan at no interest. And for the wealthiest the loans could amount to tens of thousands of dollars."[8]

Clinton's proposed tax policies certainly belied his rhetoric of "equal sacrifice for all." Rather, he seemed to be following in the footsteps of his Republican predecessor. For "equal sacrifice" to have some meaning, it would have to involve substantially increasing the flow of income from the wealthy to the middle and lower classes over the rest of the decade, thereby ensuring a return to a more equitable economy and society. Instead, the "populist" White House called for "equal sacrifice" between those who have suffered massive declines in living standards and those who had grown wealthy and affluent—courtesy of the Reagan and Bush policies.

When the Reagan White House and the Democratic Congress loosened the regulations covering banks and savings and loan institutions, they unleashed an era of greed, speculation, and mismanagement that culminated in hundreds of billions of dollars in losses by financial institutions that the U.S. government was forced to cover. Ultimately, the legislature passed a new set of regulations to monitor and control banking activity. During the electoral campaign, Clinton promised to shift the country's economic priorities toward "rebuilding America's industries," thus eliminating the conditions that led to the massive banking scandals of the previous decade. Once in office, however, the Democrats indicated a desire to undo some of the banking reforms and return to practices reminiscent of the previous era. The president's working group on "banking reform," headed by Eugene Ludwig, a prominent corporate lawyer with strong ties to the banking fraternity, recommended that banks be allowed to lend on the basis of "character" as well as collateral, and that the government should "make it easier for small banks to lend to members of their boards"[9]—precisely the kind of "insider dealings" that led to the savings and loan scandal and massive bankruptcies in the 1980s. Clinton's advisors wanted to further weaken public regulation of the banks by allowing them to appeal unfavorable decisions by federal banking examiners.

The White House rationale for pushing such deregulatory measures was "to ease the credit crunch" and "to help the economy." But the banks' failure to lend on a big scale had little to do with obstructive regulations and more to do with greater profits to be made by purchasing Treasury notes and lending abroad, and the fact that the U.S. economy was mired in a recession. Instead of "helping" the economy, the new recommendations would encourage bankers to speculate in search of higher profits and to move funds without the constraints of public accountability. They promised to severely undercut Clinton's "industrial policy."

Prior to, and following, the November presidential election, Clinton and his advisors stressed, time and again, that the Democratic administration would give top priority to "structural" problems (falling productivity, declining incomes, eroding industrial base, etc.) that plagued the American economy. "The big challenge," said Robert Reich after the election victory, "is to prevent the long-term structural agenda from being trumped by problems with the short-term business cycle."[10] As part of a "stimulus and investment" strategy, Clinton had promised to spend at least $30 billion to create new well-paid jobs and repair the nation's decaying infrastructure. But after January 1993, the focus on long-term structural changes began to take a back seat to deficit reduction. This reflected the fact that, with the exception of Reich, every one of Clinton's key economic advisors—Lloyd Bentsen, Robert Rubin, Roger Altman, Office of Management and Budget Director Leon Panetta and his deputy Alice Rivlin—were "deficit hawks."

Clinton's budget proposals reflected this post-election shift: the economic stimulus package was almost halved to around $16 billion, to be divided roughly equally between "job retraining" and infrastructure investments. Analyzing the tax, spending, and investment proposals, economist David Gordon concluded that over the next four years "the balance favors net deficit reduction over new investments by a margin of nearly two to one."[11] Even if the package had not subsequently been filibustered to defeat by Senate Republicans, it would not have come close to keeping pace with the new additions to the work force in 1993–94 alone, or compensate for the hundreds of thousands of white-collar jobs that major corporations were in the process of shedding throughout the first twelve months of the Clinton presidency.

The proposed public infrastructure spending allocation would have made little more than a dent in reversing a decade of neglect and decay. A senior administration official with responsibilities in this area estimated the cost of just making needed repairs to the nation's bridges and highways at $290 billion. Some months later, in October, with the support of Transportation Secretary Federico Peña, he proposed a solution to this particular problem: implement the Reagan-Bush idea of privatizing sections of the Interstate System to raise the necessary funds through imposing new tolls and increasing existing ones.[12]

Finally, the allocation for education and training programs in the first Clinton budget made a mockery of his campaign pledge to "put people first." Not only did the share of the economy (Gross Domestic Product) devoted to federal investment programs fall by around 2 to 3% compared with the last year of the Bush administration, education and training programs were set to experience the biggest single decline of nearly 6%.[13]

The year-long focus on deficit reduction at the expense of investments, though, has not produced a national economic recovery. New York, California, Pennsylvania, and other key states are still in recession. During 1993, according to a *U.S. News and World Report* analysis, the ten states that experienced the most gains were responsible for a mere 11% of total economic activity while the ten states where economic revival had been weakest accounted for 40%.[14]

But the subordination of domestic economic revival to deficit reduction (beginning with Clinton's endorsement of the idea that all funds raised by budget tax increases and spending cuts be used for this purpose[15]) reflected the powerful influence of the bankers and investment advisors who financed the Democratic presidential campaign and dominate the administration. It is not surprising that Clinton has pointed to the positive response of the bond market as an indicator of the success of his program. Balancing budgets (particularly at the expense of wage and salary employees) means more profits and business for bond buyers and sellers—including the investment houses represented in the Cabinet. Financiers are heartened by the prospects of the large flows of international funds and a stable dollar. Wall Street could return as a primary financial entity. Nor is it a surprise that the Reagan-appointed chairman of the Federal Reserve Bank, Alan Greenspan, strongly endorsed the Clinton economic program. Deflationary policies mean falling interest rates and rising bond prices. Spending cuts is the ideal policy for bond holders. An even more vociferous advocate of budget cuts and deficit politics has been none other than Ross Perot whose fortune is invested in bonds. The widening gap between Clinton's rhetoric and policy proposals led one commentator to astutely observe that he talks like Franklin Roosevelt but acts like Herbert Hoover.

The prevailing economic wisdom of the Reagan-Bush years was that the upward redistribution of wealth and income would result in greater investment in productive activities, creating more jobs and higher incomes for all. As we now know, nothing of the sort happened: the rich became richer, millions of well-paid jobs disappeared, and speculation flourished. Nonetheless, under Clinton a new version of "trickle-down" economics has been touted, this time taking the form of a "trickle-down technology." According to Secretary of Labor Robert Reich, state subsidies to private businesses for technological development will create high-paying jobs and also make the U.S. economy more globally competitive. The administration has budgeted $17 billion over the next four years to subsidize state-industry cooperation with the basic aim of making state research centers the "incubators" of advanced technology for corporate profitmaking.

But one of the lessons of the 1980s is that the high-tech approach and tax subsidies did not create new well-remunerated jobs. The introduction of new technologies enabled enterprises to increase productivity levels as they pared down their workforce. As demand picked up, however, the new technology combined with longer work hours and tighter discipline of labor meant that few, if any, new workers were hired. Productivity gains came at the expense of job creation.[16] In the last quarter of 1992, for instance, the economy grew between 3 and 4% while the unemployment level remained almost stationary. This trend has shown no signs of reversal since Clinton entered the White House. The case of the resurgent semiconductor industry is illustrative. It employs approximately 34,000 less workers now than it did in 1988, even though it boasts the world's leading corporation, Intel, which achieved record sales of $5.9 billion in 1992 and $8.8 billion in 1993.[17] During 1993, overtime payments in the manufacturing sector spiralled as factory owners sought to contain the rising cost of benefits they are obliged to pay their full-time workers.[18]

Measured by Gross Domestic Product, the economic upswing since 1991 has been the weakest of all postwar recoveries: the 2.7% average for the three years to December 1993 is a third below the 4.5% average of the eight earlier expansions. It has also produced fewer jobs than any other revival over the past 50 years: in 1993 alone, 600,000 mostly white collar jobs were lost to corporate "re-structuring." Furthermore, such mass sackings are set to continue. Another 108,000 positions disappeared in January 1994 as the corporate world (Eastman-Kodak, Philip Morris, NCR, etc.) fulfills its commitment to eliminate thousands more through the end of 1996.[19] Job losses and wage stagnation (see below) are the accompaniments to rising productivity and higher profits.

The 0.7% decline in the official unemployment rate during Clinton's first year in office (to 6.4%) is a deceptive indicator of any real improvement in the nation's job plight. The official rate count, for instance, excludes the 75 to 80% of black and hispanic youths living in big cities who do not even bother looking for employment. Nor does it take account of the millions of self-employed workers who are underemployed, the victims of corporate layoffs, downsizing, and slashed budgets.[20] Furthermore, in the twenty-eight months of "job recovery" since the 1990–91 recession, the net gain in payroll employment was only 563,000 compared with a 3.3 million figure for similar periods of previous postwar revivals.[21] And most of new positions continue to be lower paying and less secure than the recession-lost jobs. Between January and July 1993, 60% of new hirings were part time.[22]

Real wage levels have continued their downward trend under Clinton for almost all workers with the lowest paid sectors experiencing the most rapid loss of purchasing power. In the first half of 1993, real wages across the board declined by 0.6% compared to the first half of 1991, and they declined by 1.1% compared to the first six months of the Bush administration.[23] Moreover, the administration has failed to increase the $4.25-an-hour minimum wage (whose real value has declined over the past decade to about $2.50). In October, the strongest advocate of a minimum-wage increase, Labor Secretary Robert Reich, agreed to put his campaign "on hold" until after Congress had voted on what promised to be a long, drawn-out debate on the administration's health-care reform package. At a time when a family of three living on a full-time minimum wage were earning $2,300 below the poverty line (the same worker earned $459 above it in 1979), a *Wall Street Journal* report noted that the current $4.25 an hour "provided an income so meager that welfare recipients often do better if they turn down jobs paying it."[24] One result of falling wages has been growing homelessness. According to a survey of twenty-six major cities released by the United States Conference of Mayors, the number of families seeking food and shelter in 1993 increased by 30%; families jumped from 33% to 43% of the homeless population during the first year of the Clinton presidency.[25] So much for the election rhetoric about "putting people first."

By concentrating on capital-intensive, high-technology growth instead of labor-intensive and low-tech human social services (health, education, energy conservation, etc.), Clinton seems to be sabotaging his own "stimulus and investment" strategy. The policy of "trickle-down technology" appears to be further polarizing the nation's social structure—widening the gap between the rich high-tech capitalists and the majority of workers in low-paid, part-time service jobs, alongside a significant proportion of the workforce who have no prospects of ever finding employment again.

Clinton's domestic policy reversals since entering the White House have also extended to the formulation of a new health care policy: during 1993, the social rhetoric of the election campaign appeared to shift to a more "market" oriented approach. The call for universal health care has given way to a focus on lowering the costs of the existing health care program. In February 1993, Clinton proposed more than $38 billion of savings from projected federal health expenditures over a four-year period, including reductions in annual increases in payments to doctors and hospitals under the medicare program for the elderly and disabled. In these circumstances, however, doctors in private practice would probably be less willing to take patients paid by state programs, thus inevitably lowering the quality and scope of health care. To accommodate the powerful health insurance industry, the administration catchcry subsequently became "managed competition"—a program to be funded through payroll tax and with the market accepting some form of government regulation. In the course of the evolving debate, agreement was reached on the need to correct some major inequities in the existing system, e.g., including a benefit package to cover the tens of millions of uninsured Americans. But there was little to indicate that the proposed new approach would stop giving preferential treatment to those with most ability to pay. In September, a Harvard Medical School expert remarked that what was being proposed seemed to be moving toward "really ratifying a multi-tiered health-care system."[26] The legislation eventually submitted to Congress in 1994 was perhaps most notable for its effort to avoid any major confrontation with the dominant forces (insurance companies, pharmaceutical manufacturers, doctors, hospitals) in the industry.

One of the key planks of the Clinton campaign platform was a commitment to major reductions in military spending and a comprehensive effort to reconvert military industry to civilian production. Given the disintegration of the Soviet empire, there seemed even less reason to maintain the mammoth 1980s spending levels. But the 1994 budget approved by Congress reflected little evidence of Washington's accommodation to the changed global context: the administration's request of $263 billion, $0.5 billion less than the Pentagon's own budget recommendations, was only cut by $2.6 billion. The $261 billion authorization constitutes a fairly incremental fall (approximately $12 billion) compared with the last Republican (Bush) defense budget.[27] Furthermore, Clinton has proposed a $1.3 trillion diversion of funds to the military over the next five years, reflecting his strong support for the new Pentagon strategy of being able to fight two regional wars "nearly simultaneously."

Although the White House resisted outgoing Defense Secretary Les Aspin's request for additional funds, the president did tell his first choice to replace Aspin, former deputy director of the CIA

Bobby Ray Inman, that "whatever happened he would not seek less military spending for next year (1994) than had been previously planned."[28] After Inman declined the offer, Clinton turned to another military "hawk," the chairman of the Senate Armed Forces Committee Sam Nunn. A persistent critic of the administration's limited cuts in the defense budget, Nunn also turned down the offer of a cabinet appointment. Finally, Deputy Defense Secretary William Perry agreed to accept the job. At confirmation hearings before the Senate Armed Services Committee, Perry described himself as both a highly competent technocrat and global strategist.[29] That Clinton's search for a new Pentagon head was frustrating is, however, of less significance than the type of nominee deemed "appropriate" and the continuation of military spending at Cold War levels—affirming the basic continuity of "empire building" policies with his predecessors.

Today, the Clinton White House's level of military spending has little relevance to world politics. What it suggests is the administration's failure to construct an alternative civilian economic program capable of absorbing the displaced workers from the military-industrial complex in states like California where high-level unemployment is rife in the aerospace and other defense-related industries.

Within a relatively short period of time, the Clinton administration began redefining its political agenda on virtually every major issue of the day. Instead of social changes benefitting workers and the poor and a significant economic stimulus to revitalize industry, the emphasis shifted to a call for more "sacrifices" and a concern for deficit reduction and other deflationary policies. Instead of giving priority to enacting a universal health program, the emphasis shifted to squeezing health services in the interests of reducing the deficit. Instead of cutting taxes on wage and salaried workers, the beneficiaries of new tax concessions were real estate developers and high-tech industries. Instead of a new industrial policy, the focus shifted to a greater deregulation of the banks. Instead of promised large cuts in the military budget, projected spending levels are only marginally smaller than the Bush authorizations.

In 1994, the income disparity between rich and poor continues to widen, the purchasing power of all workers continues to fall, stable and well-paid jobs continue to disappear in the hundreds of thousands and are replaced by temporary/part-time positions, and there are significantly more homeless families in America than a year ago. This dislocating effect of these trends on the country's poor shows no signs of abating. And, like Reagan and Bush before him, Clinton's response seems remarkably similar: allocate more financial resources to incarcerate law breakers and impose "order." In April, the House passed a draconian $28 billion anti-crime bill intended to hire tens of thousands more police and build new regional prisons. It also calls for harsher sentencing measures in a nation whose prison population is already, on a percentage basis, the highest in the industrialized world. Elsewhere, the current federal budget, which includes a plan to actually reduce existing levels of social services and increase the tax burden on the poor (in order to fund new work and job training programs), has proposed a 68% increase in anti-crime funding (to $3.7 billion) over the next five years.[30]

The 1992 elections decisively repudiated the Bush administration and a decade of free-market orthodoxy, and provided the victorious Clinton forces with a powerful mandate for social change, increased public investment in the nation's physical and human infrastructure, and redistribution of wealth and income from the rich to the middle and lower classes. Thus far, the new administration has revealed itself unwilling to come to grips with fundamental causes of domestic decline that occurred during the Republican era. At best it has interspersed symbolic gratification to some popular Democratic constituencies with substantive economic concessions to elite sectors (banking, real estate, etc.), mostly large contributors to the Clinton presidential campaign. The pursuit of policies linked to global power dominate Washington's thought and action—in the process diverting new resources from the domestic economy to facilitate the spread of U.S. international capital and commerce. But there is a limit to how far the new president's populist rhetoric can mask his essentially pro-business and "global leadership" policies. Dashed hopes, broken promises, and a millionaires cabinet administering painful social policies ("sacrifices") are, potentially, the ingredients for a new political realignment at the expense of a bipartisanship that still characterizes the two-party system.

STILL THE SAME OLD GLOBAL VISION?

Like its predecessors, the Clinton administration is overseeing policies that promote the growth of the nation's global corporations at the expense of the domestic economy. State financing of military and ideological institutions abroad drain resources from social programs at home. Both "decline" and "growth" within the state and the economy coincide with different sets of class interests located in different spatial units. For bankers, CEOs, generals, commodity dealers, media moguls, and academic ideologues tied to the international circuits, it is vital to sustain "global leadership" because that is where their wealth and power is determined: for them, maintaining "global competitiveness" is a code word for lowering living standards in the domestic economy. The rhetoric that speaks to the "imperatives of the global marketplace" reflects their struggles to enhance world market shares and profits while lowering domestic social costs.

Throughout the Reagan-Bush years, policymakers evaded the profound contradiction that existed between empire building and domestic needs by referring to vague international responsibilities. This simply diverted attention from the consequences of large-scale reallocation of funds from the domestic society to overseas activities that the "empire" commitment entailed. The Republican White House, while repeatedly insisting on taking credit for establishing a "New World Order," continued to use perceived threats to this transformed globe—what Bush described as "active hostility" to "American principles"—to bludgeon the American public to accept one sacrifice in living standards after another to sustain it.

If Clinton's senior foreign policymakers had strong ties to the most influential economic forces in American society, they were also advocates of projecting power abroad and stressed the importance of continued U.S. "global leadership." Secretary of Defense Les Aspin backed aid to the Nicaraguan contras and funding of the MX missile, was a strong supporter of Operation Desert Storm, and, during early 1993, indicated a willingness to use American air power in Bosnia and force, if necessary, to gain Iraqi compliance with United Nations resolutions mandating the destruction of its nuclear and chemical arsenals. National Security Council advisor Anthony Lake was a particularly vigorous advocate of employing force in Bosnia while even the supposedly "prudent" and "cautious" Secretary of State Warren Christopher indicated during his confirmation hearings that the administration was quite prepared to use force to bolster its diplomacy. In late January 1993, he told reporters that Bosnia could well be the initial target: "[It] does seem to be a place where the United States needs to be activist and internationalist in outlook."[31] Meanwhile, CIA Director Woolsey quickly rejected calls for intelligence budget cuts in the post-Cold War era, declaring that the world was still full of forces hostile to U.S. interests, mostly located in the Third World: "We have slain the dragon. But we live now in a jungle filled with a bewildering variety of poisonous snakes."[32] The White House concurred and proceeded to wage a sustained campaign not only to avoid deep congressional cuts in the $29 billion budget but also to request a $1 billion increase in funding for fiscal 1994.[33]

During his election, and prior to his inauguration, Clinton gave unqualified endorsement to the Bush administration actions in Iraq and Somalia, argued for more forceful projections of American air power in Bosnia, and declared that he would "drop a hammer" on Cuba if he gained the presidency. Indeed, his endorsement of the Cuban Democracy Act of 1992 (the so-called Torricelli Bill) that bans subsidiaries of American corporations abroad from trading with Cuba forced a reluctant George Bush (who was demanding the harshest concessions for normalizing bilateral relations in three decades) to embrace the initiative and subsequently sign it into law.

Clinton in office has evidenced no interest in seeking to change the structural forces (economic, ideological, political) of which "empire building" is the product. In a major policy speech delivered at Johns Hopkins University in September 1993, the National Security Council's Anthony Lake spelled out the administration's global strategy of "enlargement" that seemed essentially a mirror image of the basic policy framework ("global leadership") established by the Reagan-Bush White House. "Only one overriding factor can determine whether the U.S. should act multilaterally or unilaterally, and that is America's interests," he told his audience. "We should act multilaterally where doing so advances our interests. We should act unilaterally when that will serve our purpose." He then proceeded to reaffirm the need for continued U.S. "global leadership" while implicitly acknowledging the eroding domestic support for such a posture: "Rallying Americans to bear the costs and burdens of international engagement is no less important [than in the past]. But it is much more difficult [today]. For this reason, those who recognize the value of our leadership in the world should devote far more energy to making the case for sustained engagement abroad and less energy to debates over tactics."[34]

Within this framework, the Democratic White House has pursued, even if less aggressively, the Bush global agenda. NATO was deemed still "fundamental for preserving our security;"[35] in early 1994, the president and his Secretary of State called for a greater application of NATO military power to impose a political solution on the Bosnian conflict. Using NATO to enforce regional stability in this region of post-Cold War Europe was necessary, they contended, "to vindicate United States leadership" of the Western Alliance.[36]

The administration put American troops in Somalia while keeping a military presence in Panama. In Haiti, it continued to pressure the ousted democratically elected president, Jean Bertrand Aristide, to adopt a more flexible approach toward dealing with the armed forces and the country's economic elite. Washington's "centrist" solution to the Haitian crisis is premised on shrinking Aristide's authority while ostensibly working for his return to the island. The approach has done nothing but allow the military to steadily consolidate its power through intimidation and violence. Policy toward Cuba remains hostile and unbending: it combines efforts to tighten bilateral economic sanctions and limit Havana's Western trade ties with public declarations that there can be "no accommodation, no negotiations, no normal relations"[37] in the absence of a change in regime or unless Castro "is willing to make the kind of changes that we would expect."[38] Clinton's decisive role in ensuring passage of the "Toricelli Bill" into law also affirmed the continued White House support for the doctrine of extra-territoriality.

One of the major objectives of the "enlargement" strategy is to mobilize the state's resources to promote agreements that free markets and open up economies around the world to the benefit of the U.S. overseas capitalist class. "I recently sent a message to all ambassadors," Secretary of State Christopher told a meeting of American business executives in July 1993, "making it clear that I expect each of them to take personal charge of promoting our commercial interests—and to engage their embassies in a sustained effort to help the American business community.[39] The president himself directly intervened to bring negotiations involving a multi-billion dollar U.S. airplanes and telecommunications deal with Saudi Arabia to a successful conclusion. The Treasury Department signalled that it would organize a vigorous campaign to increase U.S. access to financial services markets in key Asian and Latin American countries.

Paralleling these diplomatic initiatives has been an increased White House commitment to (direct and indirect) large-scale state subsidies in order to make American industrial corporations operating abroad more globally competitiveness. During 1993, the Overseas Private Investment Corporation received an additional $40 million to insure U.S. investments in the former Soviet Union while the Export-Import Bank was given $150 million to facilitate expanded U.S. international trade. In late September, a large number of export controls on computers and other high-technology products were terminated; the new rules exempted up to $35 billion of computer gadgetry from export-licensing requirements.[40] More recently, in April 1994, the president approved a $1 billion Defense Department program to help U.S. companies compete with Japan in making advanced flat-panel computer display screens.[41]

The administration has also waged a sustained campaign to force Japan to open up its markets to more U.S. imports. By February

1994, after eight months of negotiations, the two sides remained deadlocked over Washington's insistence that Tokyo open its markets further and set firm numerical targets to increase its purchases of American goods in order to stabilize a more than $50 billion trade imbalance. Undeterred by what they described as Japan's stubbornness, senior State and Treasury officials restated the U.S.'s "determin[ation] that there shall be greater access . . . for American businesses in the Japanese market."[42]

While full-time manufacturing positions are eliminated in droves and temporary jobs increase by an even greater number, the Clinton White House has not deviated from the Reagan-Bush policy of aggressively seeking to expand the opportunities for U.S. investors to "export jobs" abroad. In the Third World, the focus on Latin America and Asia is not happenstance: it builds on already established trends. In Latin America, U.S. investors were the major foreign beneficiaries of the regionwide "restructuring" measures and creation of "free-market" regimes during the 1980s, culminating in a 34% increase in direct investment between 1989 and 1992.[43] During this same period, U.S. direct investment in Asia jumped by 56%, more than double the increase in total overseas investment. With the advent of a Democratic administration, there has been no levelling off in this growth. American corporations have taken advantage of the current economic boom in the Chinese city of Shanghai such that by the end of 1993 they accounted for more of the $12.8 billion foreign investment stake than all other groups with the exception of Hong Kong nationals.[44]

There is no better illustration of Clinton's pursuit of policies that fulfil the goals of "empire" and multinational capital than his support for the North American Free Trade Agreement (NAFTA). Congressional passage of the legislation was achieved as a result of an embarrassing orgy of wheeling and dealing by the White House, leading one senior administration official to remark that he was "not used to being in this sewer of boutique politics."[45]

NAFTA was a Bush administration initiative that targeted Mexico because the Salinas government (1988–94) was excessively hospitable and already beginning to offer U.S. capital the most lucrative labor product and natural resource market in the hemisphere, as well as the largest number of public enterprises for takeover. Collaborating with the economic oligarchy and the powerful official trade union leadership, Salinas proceeded to force down labor costs; crush independent union initiatives on better wages, workplace conditions, and safety standards; and make labor more "flexible" and more "disciplined." In the midst of a 1992 strike of Volkswagen workers over the company's plans to lower wages and revise work rules, for example, Salinas gave permission for the company to tear up its labor contract, fire 14,000 workers, and then rehire all but several hundred "dissidents" at reduced rates of pay.[46]

Nor were productivity gains passed on in the form of higher wages. While Mexican labor productivity rose 41% between 1980 and 1992, the wages and benefits of workers were 68% at the end of this period of what they were at the beginning.[47] In 1992, the average hourly compensation, including benefits, for production-line workers in Mexico was $2.35 compared to $16.17 in the United States.[48]

U.S. investors were also attracted by the absence of basic environmental services and safeguards. In the Valley of Mexico, home to Mexico City and some 16 million people, almost nine-tenths of the waste water still goes untreated, there is a single toxic waste landfill for some 60,000 industrial companies, and there are no commercial incinerators for toxic wastes.[49]

Responding to Salinas' policies, U.S. investments have surged into Mexico in recent years. Billions flowed into the assembly plant (*maquiladora*) sector that offered the most optimal conditions for profit making: high-productivity workers and rock-bottom wages.

Salinas accelerated the elimination of tariff barriers begun by his successor de la Madrid in 1987. The major beneficiaries in this instance were also U.S. companies—those seeking greater access to the Mexican market. The subsequent surge in American exports transformed a $5.5 billion trade deficit with Mexico in 1987 into a $5.4 billion surplus in 1992. Between 1985 and 1992, U.S. exports to Mexico increased in value from $13.1 billion to $39.6 billion.[50]

Against this background, it was not surprising that American global corporations (General Electric, Du Pont, American Express, General Electric, etc.) spent millions of dollars in lobbying for NAFTA's passage through the U.S. Congress, perceiving it as "an unparalleled opportunity" for building on the gains already achieved.[51] In concert with its post-election focus on the needs of "empire" and global capital at the expense of the domestic economy, the Clinton White House wholeheartedly embraced the agreement and played *the* decisive role in ensuring a majority of votes in support of the legislation.

The agreement is certain to quicken the process of U.S. corporations undermining Mexican local producers and gaining control of local markets. In the rural sector, to encourage agricultural exports, peasants were shouldered off their traditional *ejido* holdings and replaced by giant agri-business during the Salinas era. As a result, Mexico's production of staple foods for local consumption declined, forcing it to import more of these basic items from abroad. Rural dislocation will deepen under NAFTA as more farmers are forced to compete with relatively inexpensive U.S. grain produce, especially corn, and more of their land is made legally available to foreign investors. On the other hand, NAFTA will have no impact on Mexican wage levels; nor will it lead to any amelioration in the widespread abuse of workers' rights that helped bring it about. President Clinton did negotiate a labor "side agreement" to the original treaty but the White House subsequently acknowledged that it was basically unenforceable, thus "implicitly endors[ing] the abuses inherent in the Mexican labor-relations system."[52]

The end of the Cold War has strengthened Washington's determination to consolidate its informal empire in Latin America. In the context of the relative decline in U.S. global economic power (displacement by Germany in Europe and by Japan in Asia, trade deficits with major allies), the U.S. is intensifying efforts to hold onto its favored dominion of exploitation, profits and interest payments. NAFTA is the centerpiece of a new economic strategy—based on freeing markets, exploiting labor, seizing resources, and breaking down all barriers to U.S. commerce and investment—through which Washington hopes to use the hemisphere as a springboard for its reemergence as a more competitive player in the world market.

Buoyed by the NAFTA outcome, the president arrived in Seattle in late September to preach once more the litany of open markets and elimination of trade barriers (the interests of "empire") before Western leaders of the fifteen-nation forum on Asia-Pacific Cooperation (APEC). By the end of the decade, according to one study, these nations will account for 40% of U.S. foreign trade, double that of Europe.[53] Clinton's aim in Seattle was to ensure greater U.S. accessibility to these markets in the future—especially given the $80 billion trade deficit the U.S. was currently running with APEC member countries.[54]

Over the past decade, the global economy has been a battleground for the multinationals—an arena of intense inter-capitalist competition. Witness the trade and investment rivalry between the United States and Japan in Asia.[55] On occasion, however, cooperation has taken precedence over conflict—although still at the expense of domestic producers and immobile national labor forces. This was never more evident than in the case of the third major economic agreement enthusiastically supported by the Clinton administration and American multinationals, the General Agreement on Tariffs and Trade (GATT), signed in mid-December, under which 117 nations agreed to cut their tariffs by an average of one-third. The magnitude of promised financial benefits was a powerful inducement to cooperation and compromises among the major "blocs" and their overseas capitals.[56] Global corporations (manufacturing, agricultural, high-technology, aerospace, computer software, services, etc.) headquartered in the industrialized world will reap the lion's share of the future GATT bounty. Within a decade, the total gain for multinationals based in the European Union is estimated to reach $61.3 billion annually, for those in Japan around $27 billion, and for their American counterparts almost $22 billion. Under the GATT agreement, the Third World will become an even more lucrative arena for U.S. exports, especially in agricultural foodstuffs and services (finance, high-tech consulting, insurance, etc.). At the same time, these regions will derive far less benefits from GATT over the long term than their more developed competitors. Africa is poised to lose $2.6 billion annually by 2002 while South America will do only marginally better, gaining a miniscule $0.8 billion yearly.[57]

Pursuing the Clinton global vision also demanded a continuing support for the increasingly anti-democratic Yeltsin government in Russia, based on the rapid implementation of "market reforms." In October 1993, Congress approved a new administration request for $2.5 billion in technical and humanitarian assistance, with Secretary of State Christopher describing Yeltsin as "the last best hope of stability and democracy in Russia."[58]

Toward the end of the year Washington did express momentary concern over the impact of the "shock therapy" approach being demanded by the IMF and the World Bank in return for financial aid on the political fortunes of Boris Yeltsin. Collapsing living standards and political gains by forces opposed to the nature and pace of economic reforms precipitated some criticism of the Fund's insensitivity to the social costs of its conditionality requirements. But the IMF remained steadfast in its refusal to disburse a promised $1.5 billion in the absence of "evidence" that the Yeltsin government was beginning to rein in the soaring inflation rate and massive budget deficit.[59] During an official visit to Russia in January 1994, however, Clinton reemphasized the fundamental link between rapid and sweeping market reforms and Western financial assistance. In subsequent congressional testimony, the newly appointed State Department Ambassador at Large for Russia, Strobe Talbott, issued a stern warning to the government in Moscow: any failure to press full steam ahead with economic reforms risked inflation spiralling to a level where it could "topple" the regime.[60]

Although receiving an electoral mandate based overwhelmingly on his proposed domestic agenda, Clinton as president has repeatedly called for "sacrifices" at home in the name of global leadership, stressing the U.S. role as "the world's strongest engine of growth and progress."[61] But such triumphant rhetoric obscures the very real failures of post-Cold War U.S. policy. The three major military interventions, for instance, have produced neither democracy nor viable economies: in Panama, unemployment is at an all-time high and drug-related activities are more pervasive than ever;[62] in Iraq, the brutal Saddam Hussein still rules with an iron fist while the military invasion restored the authoritarian monarchy to power in Kuwait; in Somalia, armed clans faded away when American troops appeared and resurfaced when they left. Meanwhile, the collapse of the Soviet empire has not brought peace, prosperity, and democracy but new authoritarian rulers, bloody ethnic wars, and economic depression.

Like Reagan and Bush, Clinton has sought to project U.S. global power. The continuities reflect the linkages between powerful structural forces in the state, economy, and society, and the executive branch of government—not individual miscalculations or flawed policies. But the circumstances of Clinton's election and his subsequent policy reversals may well be contributing to a growing popular reaction: Today, the negative effects of "empire" building are reinforcing domestic pressures (direct and indirect) for changing current White House priorities and restricting new initiatives abroad.

Domestic opposition has resulted in limits on new interventions (sending U.S. troops to the former Yugoslavia) and constrained increased involvement in others (Somalia) despite administration efforts to manipulate and convince the American public of a new humanitarian side to its international engagement. The initial intervention in Somalia was justified in terms of the physical and economic survival of innocent civilians caught up in a crisis between warring local parties. In the spring of 1993, the United Nations took over responsibility for the regional operation. There followed a series of decisions that saw Western efforts redirected toward military operations against the forces of local warlord General Mohammed Farah Aidid. While President Clinton sought to blame the United Nations for this subordination of humanitarian concerns to military objectives, all of the decisions that led to this shift "were repeatedly endorsed and sometimes driven by top American officials."[63] Domestic unease over this perceptible change in U.S. policy objectives erupted following the deaths of eighteen American soldiers in early October at the hands of Aidid's troops. In the legislature, senators reacted swiftly, voting to effectively cut off funding for U.S. troops by March 31, 1994. The White House agreed to the pullout date under the threat of possible new congressional demands for an even earlier withdrawal.

Nor have other attempts to overcome a manifest lack of domestic support for "sacrifices" in the cause of "enlargement" abroad been particularly successful. The most notable of these has been the White House efforts to "sell" a foreign aid bailout of the Russian government. Implicit acknowledgement of failure on this score is not hard to find. Reacting to a suggestion by Strobe Talbott that an expanded social "safety net" fund was under consideration in late December, senior administration officials swiftly discounted the likelihood of any increase in the $2.5 billion assistance package already committed for 1994.[64]

And even if the collapsing Russian economy and the rise of a kleptocracy under Boris Yeltsin is reason enough for the United States not to divert additional billions from its domestic economy to "stand by him," any new administration request is unlikely to receive an enthusiastic response on Capitol Hill. Legislators are clearly wary of being overly identified with foreign aid programs in a context of domestic "sacrifices" and no let-up in the growth of temporary employment as companies eliminate well-paid, stable jobs in the search for cheap labor beyond America's southern border.

For the American working class, the debate over NAFTA and Clinton's support of global power and international capitalist interests most graphically exposed the contradiction between Empire and Republic—between overseas expansion and domestic decay. The rise of a grass-roots labor opposition to the negative effects of "empire" building began to take shape: it was the first indication of growing popular awareness of the way in which the imperial system exploits the domestic economy to create opportunities for the multinational business community. Furthermore, American unions opposed the NAFTA agreement not only because it would trigger massive job losses and depress wage levels in the local economy; in the process, they became increasingly sensitive to the fact that the struggle for better wages, working conditions, and environmental protection in the U.S. was directly linked to the struggle for similar advances in Mexico. Consequently, NAFTA also produced the first stirrings of international class solidarity as American labor began supporting independent trade unions in Mexico. This included providing help to enable Mexican unions to organize, especially in factories owned by U.S. corporations. The United Electrical, Radio, and Machine Workers of America, that had lost almost 20% of its members because factories relocated south of the border, for example, started subsidizing organizers at General Electric company plants in Mexico.[65]

Not only is domestic failure rooted in the commitments implicit in sustaining global hegemony, but foreign policy crises are also likely to emerge from the conflicts and economic disasters that accompany the free-market policies in the East and South. Much of the post-Communist world is ruled by parochial ethnic warlords and free-market ideologues, as well as a varied assortment of authoritarian nationalists and pro-Western compradores—each vying with the other to sell off national patrimonies to Western investors while living standards plunge and social nets disappear. In this new world of affluent and conspicuous wealth, pro-Western political elites and impoverished, alienated, and downwardly mobile majorities, regional conflicts will intensify and Clinton's international responsibilities will beckon. Proliferating regional conflicts, deepening social cleavages, and heightened animosity to Western pillage could force the White House to increasingly divert more domestic resources to "regional wars" and international conflicts.

As Clinton's first year in office drew to a close, the *Wall Street Journal* heaped praise on the Democratic administration for its policy initiatives in support of national and, more particularly, outward-oriented capital: "On issue after issue [it has] come down on the side of corporate America."[66] But today, the majority of Americans want domestic economic reconstruction to take priority over global empire building. Rising economic growth rates geared to overseas expansion while the number of homeless Americans increase at an even faster pace is unacceptable. Cutbacks in public spending, urban decay, and declining living standards cannot continue. If the extension of the U.S. empire is not halted and reversed it could conceivably lead to domestic upheavals that would make the Los Angeles poor people's riot of 1992 look like a garden party, and signal the demise of the Clinton presidency.

CONCLUSION

The Clinton administration's policy choices—the apparent reversal of an electoral agenda based on reviving the domestic economy at the expense of "empire building" and his embrace of policies favoring overseas expansion—reflect the decisive power of the multinational corporation and finance capital within the U.S. political economy. They expose an adaptation to their needs and interests over and above any token populist flourishes in the direction of the president's voting constituency. Clinton's major cabinet appointees and policies testify to the dominant role that multinational and finance capital play in shaping the national political agenda, independent of which of the two parties occupy the White House. If the allocation of senior positions reflects the power of the dominant economic class it also highlights the way in which the state reinforces the duality of the U.S. economy by opening up new investment opportunities in Mexico, Asia, Russia, and elsewhere. The willingness of the Clinton White House to pursue the same basic policies as characterized the Republican presidencies of Ronald Reagan and George Bush have, as a consequence, led to the same polarization between the growth of overseas power and continuation of domestic decay.

At the same time, the "contradictions" of empire become more and more visible—if not to the White House, then certainly to an expanding sector of the American populace. The growing demand of multinational corporations (MNCs) for "equality" with global competitors is leading to greater "inequalities" in the domestic economy; state subsidies to enable the MNC to "compete" in the global market have gone hand in hand with a deregulated local economy that has meant falling wages, disappearing benefits, declining services, and increased diversion of funds for policing purposes (an added cost for wage and salaried groups)—in practice, the transfer of income from the national workforce to outward-looking capital. A related contradiction is between the need to exploit the domestic state to expand internationally and the declining resources of the state to finance multinational capital expansion. A third contradiction is between multinational capital's need for only a narrow educated labor force to ensure its growth and the demands of the majority of the electorate, that is, the imperatives of democratic legitimacy. Another is the widening gap between U.S. political, ideological, and military power to establish client regimes and the capacity to sustain these regimes (to provide the basis for future exploitation?). The miniscule 1994 foreign aid packages for Central American allies is particularly illustrative of this dilemma confronting U.S. policymakers.

Democratic White House efforts to accommodate the greater demands of capital to exploit the world market through the transfer of domestic resources has begun to generate growing popular discontent: opposition to NAFTA, to U.S. intervention in Somalia, to an expanded foreign aid program for Yeltsin's Russia, and to the two-party system and the politicians' failure to combat rising crime and urban decay, are some of its manifestations. To continue to focus exclusively on the "domestic causes" of domestic problems, and to proffer solutions that do not confront the economic power configuration that supports "empire building," as the Clinton administration is doing, promises to accelerate popular discontent and trigger the emergence of new political alternatives.

CONCLUSION

In the 1990s, inter-capitalist economic conflict and competition—the pursuit of global market share—has overshadowed class conflict, replaced the Cold War, and displaced the North-South conflict. The former Communist countries have been converted from adversaries into one of the regions where the competition between the new global hegemony is played out. Third World regimes have been recruited as labor and mineral reserves and manufacturing export platforms for the United States, Germany, and Japan. The world market is the terrain of conflict and competition of the dominant classes of each hegemonic power.

The United States as a global competitor has secured military and ideological preeminence on the basis of its massive state expenditures and extensive overseas networks. It has stretched its legal code to legitimate the sovereignty of its law over and above those of weaker nation states. U.S. multinational corporations have increased their worldwide investments, trade, and profits, not least as a result of their power and influence over the national political class—that has allowed them to draw lavishly on state resources (subsidies, tax concessions, incentives) and profits to finance their overseas activities.

To understand the United States today, however, requires that we recognize the bifurcation of power and wealth—between the national and international corporate economy, between global military and ideological hegemony and economic power. The U.S.

national economy and society is deteriorating: industry and manufacturing is declining; budgets and trade deficits are increasing; the foreign debt is growing; new, serious problems beset the health and education systems; social budgets are being cut to the bone; the large central cities are crumbling; the labor force is increasingly composed of low-paid, insecure workers with no social protection or visible on-the-job representatives to protect them from employer abuses. While inequalities between the international corporate elite and the burgeoning temporary labor force widen, the polarized class structure and the deep ties between the executive branch and the outward-oriented elite limit the prospects for any shift in priorities within the existing two-party system.

Class cohesion and political representation and leadership at the top is matched by political unease and insecurity in the middle and a social malaise at the bottom. The 1992 presidential protest vote for Ross Perot exposed middle-class concerns; nationwide working-class opposition to NAFTA testified to a rising political discontent over the Clinton administration's subordination of domestic economic needs to empire-oriented politics. Will class warfare from above provoke a similar response from below if the priorities are not reversed?

Class divisions persist and have become accentuated in the United States. The classes of empire, the electronic movers of capital world-wide, are anchored in the international circuits while the classes of the republic are rooted in vulnerable and immobile national communities. Today the politics of empire (Bush's "global leadership," Clinton's "enlargement") monopolize the political agenda: global actors permeate the Democratic and Republican parties and their political leaderships.

But the national economy is straining to the limits to support global power. Military and ideological supremacy cannot count on unlimited state resources and overseas capital to sustain it. These global structures that have facilitated the outflow of capital confront a shrinking revenue and tax base. State budget transfers in the form of overseas subsidies, loans, and military spending have sapped domestic programs. Moreover, in the present context, military and ideological dominance is not conducive to accumulating advantages in the New World Order. But the elites linked to the new international circuits continue to shape the political agenda. Under their influence, economists pontificate on the "global imperatives" and media pundits highlight the need for greater "international competitiveness"—to induce greater productivity, lower wages, and new large state transfers from social programs to corporate subsidies.

The problem of U.S. "decline" is not due to unfair Japanese competition or inability to "obtain real, even access to the Japanese market";[1] nor does it stem from the failure of American institutions: the multinationals *are investing* . . . overseas. It is the success of the nation's elites in converting the domestic economy into a trampoline for global leadership that has seriously undermined the domestic foundations of state power and eroded domestic society. It is not a question of "saving and investing" in the abstract or merely converting military to civilian production, but rather of transforming the state—from an imperial to a republican state—and that means confrontation with the major political parties, banks, and corporations that have profited from the exploitation of American society and the public treasury in the name of global leadership.

NOTES

INTRODUCTION

1. Joseph N. Nye, Jr., *Bound to Lead* (New York: Basic Books, 1990), passim. Henry R. Nau, *The Myth of America's Decline* (New York: Oxford University Press, 1990), especially pp. 3–49.

2. Joseph N. Nye, Jr., "No, the U.S. Isn't in Decline," *New York Times*, October 3, 1990, p. 33.

3. Paul Kennedy, *The Rise and Fall of the Great Powers* (New York: Random House, 1987).

4. See Seymour Melman, *The Permanent War Economy* (New York: Touchstone/Simon & Schuster, 1976 and 1985 editions).

5. Harry Magdoff and Paul M. Sweezy, *The End of Prosperity: The American Economy in the 1970s* (New York: Monthly Review Press, 1977); *The Deepening Crisis of U.S. Capitalism* (New York: Monthly Review Press, 1981); *Stagnation and Financial Explosion* (New York: Monthly Review Press, 1987).

1. REVIVING THE WORLD OF THE 1950s? THE U.S. AND ASCENDING GLOBAL POWER IN THE 1990s

1. Abraham F. Lowenthal, "Latin America: Ready for Partnership?" *Foreign Affairs* 72, no. 1 (1992): 77.

2. Stewart Sutely, "The Revitalization of United States Aterritorial International Logic: The World Before and After the 1989 Invasion of Panama," *Canadian Journal of Political Science* 25 no. 3 (September 1992): 440–48.

3. Linda Greenhose, "High Court Backs Seizing Foreigner for Trial in U.S.," *New York Times*, June 16, 1992, pp. 1, 12.

4. Quoted in Ian Williams, "U.S. Takeover At the U.N.," *The Nation*, October 12, 1992, pp. 392, 394. Also see Craig R. Whitney, "More Than

Ever, U.S. Policing is an American Show," *New York Times*, January 17, 1993, p. E3.

5. John Cushman Jr., "The Coming Crunch for the Military Budget," *New York Times*, November 27, 1988, p. 1E. U.S. Arms Control and Disarmament Agency, *World Military Expenditures & Arms Transfers 1990*, p. 85. U.S. Bureau of the Census, *Statistical Abstract of the United States 1992* (Washington, D.C.: U.S. Government Printing Office, 1992), p. 336.

6. Ibid.

7. David E. Sanger, "For Japan, Military Challenge is Balancing Might and Image," *New York Times*, March 6, 1989, pp. 1, 6. Michael Wines, "Allies Still Lag on Arms, U.S. Says," *New York Times*, April 18, 1990, p. 11. Doyle McManus and Jim Mann, "Big 3 Tested: Will Economic Rivalry Break Up the Allies?" *Los Angeles Times*, June 9, 1992, p. A16.

8. Quoted in Richard L. Berke, "Peace Dividend: Casualty in the Gulf?" *New York Times*, August 30, 1990, p. 14.

9. Tim Weiner, *Blank Check: The Pentagon's Black Budget* (New York: Warner Books, 1990), p. 5.

10. Patrick E. Tyler, "The Task: Slip Spies Into the New World Order," *New York Times*, May 19, 1991, p. E5.

11. Quoted in Ibid.

12. Elaine Sciolino, "Soviet Upheaval Injects Urgency into U.S. Debate on Intelligence," *New York Times*, September 2, 1991, pp. 1, 7.

13. Quoted in "Should the CIA Start Spying for Corporate America?" *Business Week*, October 14, 1991, p. 96. Also see Elaine Sciolino, "C.I.A. Casting About for New Missions," *New York Times*, February 4, 1992, pp. 1, 8.

14. Laurein Alexandre, "Anticommunism and the Voice of America: The Radio's Raison D'Etre," in Laurein Alexandre, ed. *The Ideology of International Communications* (New York: Institute for Media Analysis, 1992), p. 25.

15. For a splendid discussion, see Robert Parry and Peter Kornbluh, "Iran-Contra's Untold Story," *Foreign Policy* 72 (Fall 1988): 3–30.

16. See, for example, Douglas Farah, "Central America Feels Abandoned by Bush at Crucial Time," *Washington Post*, November 22, 1992, pp. A31, A38.

17. Thomas L. Friedman, "As Food Airlift Starts, Baker Hints U.S. Might Agree to Role in a Ruble Fund," *New York Times*, February 11, 1992, p. 14.

18. Speech by Secretary of State George Shultz, January 9, 1989, "Shultz Ends Stewardship Optimistic About World Situation," *Official Text*, U.S. Information Service, January 11, 1989.

19. Lawrence S. Eagleburger, *Unchartered Waters: U.S. Foreign Policy in a Time of Transition*, Samuel D. Berger Memorial Lecture, Georgetown University, September 13, 1989 (transcript).

20. Excerpts from the February DPG draft reprinted in Patrick E. Tyler,

"U.S. Strategy Plan Calls for Insuring No Rivals Develop," *New York Times*, March 8, 1992, p. 14.

21. Ibid.

22. Ibid.

23. Ibid.

24. Ibid.

25. See William Drozdiak and Ann Devroy, "Bush Challenges Europeans to Define U.S. NATO Role," *Washington Post*, November 8, 1991, p. A29. William Drozdiak, "U.S.-French Tension Called Peril to Alliance," *Washington Post*, May 27, 1992, p. A21.

26. Excerpts from the February DPG draft reprinted in Tyler, "U.S. Strategy Plan Calls for Insuring No Rivals Develop," p. 14.

27. Ibid.

28. Ibid.

29. Ibid.

30. Ibid.

31. Ibid.

32. Ibid.

33. Quoted in Barton Gellman, "Aim of Defense Plan Supported by Bush," *Washington Post*, March 12, 1992, p. A18.

34. See Patrick E. Tyler, "Senior U.S. Officials Assail Lone-Superpower Policy," *New York Times*, March 11, 1992, p. 6.

35. Excerpts from the April DPG draft reprinted in Barton Gellman, "Pentagon's 6-Year Plan Drops Controversial Goal," *Washington Post*, May 24, 1992, pp. A1, A23.

36. Quoted in Ibid., p. A23.

37. Ibid.

38. President George Bush, "America Must Remain Engaged," reprinted in U.S. Department of State, *Dispatch*, December 21, 1992, pp. 893–95. Also see Michael Wines, "Bush, in Texas Valedictory, Defends His Foreign Policies," *New York Times*, December 16, 1992, pp. 1, 25.

39. See William Drozdiak, "Tensions Between France and U.S. Said to Turn Allies into Rivals," *Washington Post*, January 22, 1992, p. A25. Drozdiak, "U.S.-French Tension Called Peril to Alliance," p. A21.

40. Quoted in Ibid.

41. For a discussion, see Wolfram F. Hanrieder, *Germany, America, Europe* (New Haven: Yale University Press, 1989).

2. THE DECLINE OF U.S. ECONOMIC POWER AT HOME AND ABROAD

1. See, for example, Barry Bluestone and Bennet Harrison, *Corporate Flight: The Causes and Consequences of Economic Dislocation* (Washington, D.C.: Progressive Alliance, 1981).

2. See Allen J. Scott and Michael Storper, *High Technology and Rural Development: A Theoretical Critique and Reconstruction* (London: University of Reading, 1986).

3. Joel M. Stern, et al., eds., *Corporate Restructuring and Executive Compensation* (Cambridge, MA: Ballinger, 1989), p. 138 (Table 1).

4. *Forbes'* estimates are just that. For a discussion of their technique, see *Forbes 400*, October 28, 1985. On the rising power of speculative wealth during the 1980s, also see Christopher Niggle, "Monetary Policy and Changes in Income Distribution," *Journal of Economic Issues* 23, no. 3 (September 1989): 814–15, 819.

5. Leo Troy, *Almanac of Business and Industrial Financial Ratios*, vols. 1983–89 (Englewood Cliffs, NJ: Prentice Hall).

6. David J. Ravenscraft and F.M. Scherer, *Mergers, Sell-Offs, and Economic Efficiency* (Washington, D.C.: The Brookings Institution, 1987), p. 190.

7. Quoted in Stern, et al., eds., *Corporate Restructuring and Executive Compensation*, p. 119.

8. Quoted in Ibid., p. 169.

9. See "What's Wrong With the American Economy?" *Business Week* November 2, 1992, p. 43. Gary W. Shorter and Kevin F. Winch, *Leveraged Buyouts*, Congressional Research Service Issue Brief, June 22, 1989, p. 1, 3.

10. Jerry Knight, "Buttressing the Big Banks," *Washington Post*, October 27, 1991, p. H1. "What's Wrong With the American Economy?" p. 43.

11. John Miller, "Hard Times for Bankers," *Dollars & Sense* 169 (September 1991): 6.

12. See *Binghamton Press and Sun-Bulletin*, September 24, 1989, p. 4E.

13. Michael Quint, "After Losing Ground in U.S. Citicorp Seeks Future Abroad," *New York Times*, January 20, 1992, pp. D1, D3. "What's Wrong With the American Economy?" p. 43. Michael Quint, "Bank Losses Worst in 50 Years, But No Danger to System is Seen," *New York Times*, February 17, 1991, p. 34. Eric N. Berg, "Dark Cloud of Acrimony Over World Debt Crisis," *New York Times*, May 21, 1987, pp. 1, D6.

14. James Bates, "Banks at the Barricades," *Los Angeles Times*, September 23, 1990, p. D3.

15. Michael Quint, "Bank Losses Worst in 50 Years, But No Danger to System Seen," pp. 34–35.

16. Lawrence G. Franko, "Global Corporate Competition II: Is the Large American Firm an Endangered Species?" *Business Horizons* 34, no. 6 (November–December, 1991): 15.

17. "The Global Giants," *Wall Street Journal*, September 20, 1991, p. R9. Bates, "Banks at the Barricades," p. D3.

18. Michael Quint, "U.S. Banks Cut Global Business As Rivals Grow," *New York Times*, July 5, 1990, p. D9.

19. See Paul Starobin, "Will the Banks be Next," *National Journal*,

December 30, 1989, p. 3091. Clyde V. Prestowitz, Jr., *Trading Places* (New York: Basic Books, 1989), p. 69.

20. U.S. General Accounting Office, *Foreign Investment: Aspects of the U.S.-Japan Relationship*, GAO/NSIAD–90–203FS, July 1990, p. 6.

21. See "It's Gloves-Off Time," *U.S. News and World Report*, December 25, 1989, pp. 41–42.

22. See Stephen D. Cohen, *Cowboys and Samurai: Why the United States is Losing the Industrial Battle and Why it Matters* (New York: HarperBusiness, 1991), pp. 89–93. Prestowitz, Jr., *Trading Places*, pp. 294–303. Bernard Eccelston, "The State, Finance and Industry in Japan," in Andrew Cox, ed., *State, Finance and Industry* (Brighton: Wheatsheaf Books, 1986), pp. 69–70.

23. Quoted in Paul Blustein, "Japan's Corporate Connections Create Challenge for U.S. Businesses," *Washington Post*, October 6, 1991, pp. A1, A35.

24. Fernand Protzman, "Mighty German Banks Face Curb," *New York Times*, November 7, 1989, p. D6. Also see Kenneth Dyson, "The State, Banks and Industry: The West German Case," in Cox, *State, Finance and Industry*, pp. 125–34. Herbert Oberbeck and Martin Maethge, "Computer and Pinstripes: Financial Institutions," in Peter J. Katzenstein, ed., *Industry and Politics in West Germany* (Ithaca: Cornell University Press, 1989), pp. 275–303.

25. See, for instance, Keith Bradsher, "House Blocks Spending on Savings Rescue," *New York Times*, April 2, 1992, p. D1.

26. "How to Get America Growing Again," *Business Week* (Special Issue "Reinventing America") 1992, p. 34.

27. Quoted in Donald L. Bartlett and James B. Steele, "Why the World is Closing In on the U.S. Economy," *Philadelphia Inquirer*, October 23, 1991, p. 13A.

28. Steven Mufson, "Debt Spree Leaves a Painful Legacy," *Washington Post*, September 27, 1992, pp. A1, A18. Robert D. Hershey, Jr., "Why Economists Fear the Deficit," *New York Times*, May 26, 1992, pp. D1, D3. Felix Rohatyn, "American Economic Dependence," *Foreign Affairs* 67, no. 1 (1989): 60.

29. Robert A. Blecker, *Still a Debtor Nation*, Briefing Paper, Economic Policy Institute, Washington, D.C., July 1991, p. 11. Steven Mufson, "The Political Path to a Debt Crisis," *Washington Post*, September 28, 1992, p. A8.

30. Michael Wolff, "Walking Small at Munich," *Washington Post*, July 5, 1992, p. C8.

31. Mufson, "Debt Spree Leaves a Painful Legacy," pp. A1, A18.

32. David E. Rosenbaum, "Of Budgets and Truth," *New York Times*, January 31, 1990, p. 25. Ernest F. Hollings, "Deceit, Danger and the Deficit," *New York Times*, October 5, 1990, p. 37.

33. David R. Francis, "US Finally Sheds Image As an Exporting 'Wimp'," *Christian Science Monitor* (International Weekly Edition), April

3–9, 1992, p. 10A. William H. Cooper, "U.S.-Japanese Trade," *Congressional Research Service Review*, February–March 1992, p. 21. Andrew Pollack, "Japan's Rising Trade Surpluses," *New York Times*, July 4, 1992, p. 33. Stuart Auerbach, "U.S. Trade Gap Near Highs Despite Record Exports," *Washington Post*, November 19, 1992, p. A16. Pilita Clark, "Hard Questions as Bill Begins Soft Sell," *Sydney Morning Herald*, February 20, 1993, p. 17.

34. Ronald E. Yates, "U.S. Not the Swiftest in the Race to Compete," *San Francisco Examiner*, July 2, 1992, pp. E1, E6.

35. David E. Sanger, "A Detroit Still Depends on Japan," *New York Times*, February 27, 1992, pp. 1, 10. *Christian Science Monitor*, January 5, 1990, p. 6. Bryan Boswell, "U.S. Car-Makers on Collusion Course with Japan," *The Australian*, January 26, 1993, p. 10.

36. See Franko, "Global Corporate Competition II: Is the Large American Firm an Endangered Species?" pp. 14–22.

37. Lester C. Thurow, *Head to Head: The Coming Economic Battle Among Japan, Europe, and America* (New York: William Morrow, 1992), p. 30.

38. T. R. Reid, "U.S. Again Leads in Computer Chips," *Washington Post*, November 20, 1992, pp. A1, A42. Graeme Browning, "Technies in Cahoots," *National Journal*, July 6, 1991, p. 1688.

39. Stuart Auerbach, "U.S. Relied on Foreign-Made Parts for Weapons," *Washington Post*, March 25, 1991, pp. A16, A17.

40. Andrew Pollack, "Pillar of Chip Industry Eroding," *New York Times*, March 3, 1989, p. D5.

41. Bruce Stokes, "Tooling Up," *National Journal*, October 19, 1991, pp. 2544–45, 2548. The quote is from Daniel F. Burton, Jr., Executive Vice-President of the Washington-based Council on Competitiveness.

42. U.S. Congress, Senate, Joint Economic Committee, *The 1992 Joint Economic Report*, 102nd Congress, 2nd Session, March 31, 1992 (Washington, D.C.: U.S. Government Printing Office, 1992), p. 26.

43. Dr. Francis Narin, president of CHI Research Inc. of New Jersey which compiled the study, quoted in William J. Broad, "In the Realm of Technology, Japan Looms Ever Larger," *New York Times*, May 28, 1991, p. C1; also see p. C8.

44. U.S. Congress, *The 1992 Joint Economic Report*, p. 26.

45. "Can America Compete?" *The Economist*, January 18, 1992, p. 42. Robert T. Green and Trina L. Larsen, "Changing Patterns of U.S. Trade: 1985–1989," *Business Horizons* 34, no.6 (November–December 1991): 8. John Jelacic, "The U.S. Trade Outlook in 1991," *Business America*, April 6, 1992, p. 4. Francis, "US Finally Sheds Image As an Exporting 'Wimp'," p. 10A.

46. "The Toughest Companies in America," *U.S. News & World Report*, October 28, 1991, pp. 66, 73. "Grabbing New World Orders," *Business Week* (Special issue "Reinventing America") 1992, p. 112. Patrick

Oster, "U.S. Electronic Products Plug in to Western Europe," *Washington Post*, February 23, 1992, p. H1.

47. Reid, "U.S. Again Leads in Computer Chips," pp. A1, A42. Andrew Pollack, "U.S. Chip Makers Stem the Tide in Trade Battles with Japanese," *New York Times*, April 9, 1992, pp. 1, D6.

48. Quoted in William D. Hartung, "Arms Sales Win Votes and Little Else," *New York Times*, October 25, 1992, p. F11. Also see Eric Schmitt, "Arms Makers' Latest Tune: 'Over There, Over There'," *New York Times*, October 4, 1992, p. F5.

49. Stuart Auerbach, "The U.S. as Exporter: Superpower or Subpar?" *Washington Post*, September 20, 1992, p. H1.

50. Evelyn Richards, "U.S. Firms Stage Competitive Revival," *Washington Post*, May 20, 1991, p. A8.

51. Quoted in Mufson, "Falling Dollar, Falling Stature?" *Washington Post*, August 30, 1992, p. H4. Also see Stuart Auerbach, "The U.S. as Exporter: Superpower of Subpar?" p. H1.

52. "Can America Compete?" pp. 61–62. James Sterngold, "American Business Starts a Counterattack in Japan," *New York Times*, February 24, 1992, p. D4.

53. "Can America Compete?" pp. 61–62. Sterngold, "American Business Starts a Counterattack in Japan," p. D4.

54. William J. Broad, "Japan Seen Passing U.S. in Research by Industry," *New York Times*, February 25, 1992, pp. C1, C10. David E. Sanger, "Japan's Lead in Computer Research Grows," *New York Times*, February 21, 1990, pp. D1, D4.

55. See William J. Broad, "U.S. Panel Asks More for Science," *New York Times*, August 13, 1992, p. D6.

56. "It's Gloves-Off Time," p. 41. Jeff Faux and Todd Schafer, **Increasing Public Investment**, Briefing Paper, Economic Policy Institute, Washington, D.C., October 1991, p. 10. "Industrial Policy," *Business Week*, April 6, 1992, p. 72. "How to Get America Growing Again," p. 35.

57. Faux and Schafer, **Increasing Public Investment**, pp. 10, 11. Cohen, *Cowboys and Samurai*, p. 103.

58. U.S. Congress, *The 1992 Joint Economic Report*, p. 10. Broad, "Japan Seen Passing U.S. in Research by Industry," p. C1. Wolff, "Walking Small at Munich," p. C8.

59. U.S. Congress, *The 1992 Joint Economic Report*, p. 11.

60. See, for example, Larry Q. Nowels, "Japan's Foreign Aid Program: Adjusting to the Role of the World's Leading Donor," in U.S. Congress, Joint Economic Committee, *Japan's Economic Challenge*, Study Papers, Committee Print, 101st Congress, 2nd Session, October 1990 (Washington, D.C.: U.S. Government Printing Office, 1990), pp. 398–399. "Generosity Has Its Limits," *Far Eastern Economic Review*, June 20, 1992, p. 62. Steve Coll, "Japan's Hands-On Foreign Aid," *Washington Post*, January 13, 1991, p. H1.

61. "Globalization—To What End?," *Monthly Review* 43, no. 10 (March 1992): 9.

62. Cohen, *Cowboys and Samurai*, p. 107.

63. U.S. Congress, *The 1992 Joint Economic Report*, pp. 28–29.

64. Paul Starobin, "Nation of Spenders," *National Journal*, July 21, 1991, p. 1787.

65. Congressional Research Service, *CRS Review*, June 1989, p. 19. U.S. Congress, *The 1992 Joint Economic Report*, pp. 2, 5.

66. Congressional Research Service, *CRS Review*, p. 19. "Industrial Policy," p. 72.

67. Laurent Carroue, "The Growing Strength of Germany—East and West," *Guardian Weekly* (*Le Monde* Supplement), August 26, 1990, p. 16.

68. Bruce Stokes, "East Bloc Pot of Gold?" *National Journal*, February 10, 1990, pp. 313–314.

69. Quoted in Marc Fisher, "Germany Set to Dominate East European Economies," *Guardian Weekly*, February 23, 1992, p. 17. Also see James Rupert, "Europeans Lead U.S. in Exploring Ex-Soviet Investment Frontier," *Washington Post*, February 20, 1992, p. A20.

70. Steve Lohr, "Fixing Corporate America's Short-Term Mind-Set," *New York Times*, September 2, 1992, p. D5.

71. See "It's Gloves-Off Time," p. 42.

72. "The Global Economy: Who Gets Hurt," *Business Week*, August 19, 1992, p. 53. "Smart Work," *The Economist*, August 22, 1992, p. 21.

73. Quoted in Congressional Research Service, Report to Congress, *Technological Advancement and U.S. Industrial Competitiveness*, October 28, 1988, p. 21.

74. See Louis Ferleger and Jay R. Mandle, "Co-Signs and Derivations of America's Two-Score Decline: Poor Math Skills, Poor Productivity Growth," *Challenge*, May–June 1992, p. 49.

75. Donald L. Bartlett and James B. Steele, "Why the World is Closing in on the U.S. Economy," *Philadelphia Inquirer*, October 23, 1991, p. 13A.

76. "How to Get America Growing Again," p. 35.

77. "Smart Work," p. 21.

78. Peter J. Katzenstein, "Stability and Change in the Emerging Third Republic," in Katzenstein, ed., *Industry and Politics in West Germany*, p. 335.

79. Quoted in "'What I have said is what I Feel. . . .'," *The Australian*, February 5, 1992, p. 6.

80. Bruce Stokes, "Multiple Allegiances," *National Journal*, November 11, 1989, p. 2755.

81. "Manufacturing Goes Abroad," *Christian Science Monitor*, February 14, 1991, p. 7. "Globalization—To What End?," *Monthly Review* 43, no. 9 (February 1992): 11–16. "Economic Trends," *Business Week*, September 20, 1993, p. 22.

82. Raymond J. Mataloni, Jr., "Capital Expenditures by Majority-Owned Foreign Affiliates of U.S. Companies, Latest Plans for 1991," *Survey of Current Business* 71, no. 3 (March 1991): 26. Mahnaz Fahim-Nadir, "Capital Expenditures by Majority-Owned Affiliates of U.S. Companies, Plans for 1992," *Survey of Current Business* 72, no. 3 (March 1992): 44. "Manufacturing Goes Abroad," p.7. "Globalization—To What End?," pp. 11–16.

83. "America Still Buys the World," *The Economist*, September 17, 1988, p. 78. "How to Get America Growing Again," p. 30.

84. Stokes, "Multiple Allegiances," p. 2756.

85. "How to Get America Growing Again," p. 30.

86. Stuart Auerbach and Edward Cody, "Boom Over the Border: U.S. Firms go to Mexico," *Washington Post*, May 17, 1992, p. A28. Robert A. Blecker and William E. Spriggs, *Manufacturing Employment in North America*, Briefing Paper, Economic Policy Institute, Washington, D.C., October 5, 1992, pp. 1–2.

87. Timothy Keochlin and Mehrene Larudee, "The High Cost of NAFTA," *Challenge*, September–October 1992, p. 19.

88. Keith Bradsher, "Global Issues Weigh on Town As Factory Heads to Mexico," *New York Times*, September 1, 1992, p. D4.

89. "Delivering the Goods," *Business Week*, July 13, 1992, p. 52.

90. Keochlin and Larudee, "The High Cost of NAFTA," pp. 19–20, 24.

91. Quoted in Doyle McManus, "U.S. Aid Agency Helps To Move Jobs Overseas," *Los Angeles Times*, September 28, 1992, p. A12.

92. Rebecca Smith, "Creating Foreign Jobs at Taxpayer Expense," *Philadelphia Inquirer*, October 8, 1992, pp. C9, C10. Jack Sheinkman, "How Washington Exports U.S. Jobs," *New York Times*, October 18, 1992, p. F13.

93. "It's Gloves-Off Time," p. 42.

94. David R. Francis, "Advice to Excess: 'Think Globally'," *Christian Science Monitor*, April 11, 1991, p. 9. Stokes, "Multiple Allegiances," p. 2756.

95. "Locking Up Tomorrow's Profits," *U.S. News and World Report*, June 29, 1992, p. 58. "For GM, The Word from Europe is 'Parts'," *Business Week*, January 18, 1993, p. 53. "What's Wrong With the American Economy," *Business Week*, November 2, 1992, p. 39.

96. David E. Sanger, "Power of the Yen Winning Asia," *New York Times*, December 5, 1991, p. D22.

97. "Carving Out a Place in the Pacific Century," *Business Week*, November 11, 1991, p. 66.

98. Bruce Stokes, "Japan's Asia Edge," *National Journal*, June 29, 1991, p. 1624. Japan's trade surplus with South and East Asia increased by approximately 33% to $37.4 billion in 1991. Pollack, "Japan's Rising Trade Surpluses," p. 33.

99. Bruce Stokes, "Driving East," *National Journal*, November 14,

1992, pp. 2515–16. William Branigan, "Effort Planned to Boost American Trade in Asia," *Washington Post*, March 20, 1992, p. A20.

100. "Japanese MNCs Shift Offshore Investment Focus to Manufacturing in 1988," *Business International*, October 16, 1989, p. 318. "Finance and Service Sectors Power Japan's Offshore Capital Flows in 1989," *Business International*, August 13, 1990, p. 271. Steven Greenhouse, "Agonizing Over Japan," *New York Times*, April 30, 1989, pp. F1, F8.

101. Bruce Stokes, "Staking Out Europe," *National Journal*, May 25, 1991, p. 1228. Barbara Rudolph, "Ducking in the Cross Fire," *Time*, February 10, 1992, p. 15. Pollack, "Japan's Rising Trade Surpluses," p. 33.

102. Roger Cohen, "U.S. Unable to Lead Europe out of a Slump," *New York Times*, April 7, 1992, p. D1.

103. Cohen, *Cowboys and Samurai*, p. 171.

104. See Paul Blustein, "Tariffs Not the Key to Japanese Markets," *Washington Post*, January 4, 1992, pp. B1, B6.

105. Cohen, *Cowboys and Samurai*, p. 172.

106. See David E. Sanger, "In Japan's View, U.S. Car Companies Should Be Blaming Only Themselves," *New York Times*, January 6, 1992, p. 12. Sanger, "A Detroit Still Depends on Japan," pp. 1, 10.

107. A number of influential academic studies have also propagated the argument that Japan discriminates against foreign exporters. See, for example, Prestowitz, Jr., *Trading Places*; and James Fallows, *More Like Us* (New York: Holmes & Meier, 1990).

108. See James K. Jackson, "Japan's Financial Stake in the United States: How Stable is It?" in U.S. Congress, *Japan's Economic Challenge*, pp. 190, 196. "Lost Incentives," *Business Week*, June 25, 1992, p. 53. James Sterngold, "Japanese Shifting Investment Flow Back toward Home," *New York Times*, March 22, 1992, p. 12. "Reversal of Fortune," *U.S. News and World Report*, February 17, 1992, p. 43. Kirstin Downey, "Japanese Slow Real Estate Buying Spree," *Washington Post*, February 21, 1992, pp. F1, F2. "Japan Ties up the Asian Market," *The Economist*, April 24, 1993, p. 27.

3. EXTERNAL EXPANSION AND INTERNAL DECAY: THE DIALECTICS OF GLOBAL POWER

1. Thomas B. Edsall, *Chain Reaction* (New York: W.W. Norton, 1991), p. 23. Data compiled by the Congressional Budget Office, in Sylvia Nasar, "Even Among the Well-Off, the Rich Get Richer," *New York Times*, March 5, 1992, p. 1. U.S. Congress, Joint Economic Committee, Democratic Staff Study, *Falling Behind: The Growing Income Gap in America*, November 1, 1990, pp. 2–4.

2. Donald L. Bartlett and James B. Steele, "How the Game was Rigged Against the Middle Class," *Philadelphia Inquirer*, October 20, 1991, p.

16A. Also see Paul Farhi, "Number of U.S. Millionares Soars," *Washington Post*, July 11, 1992, p. A1.

3. Kevin Phillips, *The Politics of Rich and Poor* (New York: Random House, 1990), p. 207.

4. *Boston Globe*, October 21, 1990, p. A21.

5. Paul Taylor, "Study Finds Income Growth Rate of Two-Parent Families Fell Sharply in 1980s," *Washington Post*, January 17, 1992, p. A15.

6. Edsall, *Chain Reaction*, pp. 194, 195. U.S. Congress, *The 1992 Joint Economic Report*, p. 42.

7. See Nasar, "Even Among the Well-Off, the Rich Get Richer," p. D24.

8. Robert J. McCartney, "Executive Pay Rises, as Profits Fall," *Washington Post*, April 25, 1992, pp. C1, C6. "U.S Fat Cats Defy Slump for a Mean $5.3m Salary," *The Australian*, April 17–18, 1993, p. 9.

9. Steve Lohr, "Amid Layoffs and the Recession, Executives' Pay is Under Scrutiny," *New York Times*, January 20, 1992, p. D8.

10. David E. Sanger, "In Japan's Bad Times, Chiefs Say Sorry and Cut Their Pay," *New York Times*, April 11, 1992, pp. 1, 42. The Standard & Poor's and Towers Perrin studies are referred to in McCartney, "Executive Pay Rises, as Profits Fall," pp. C1, C6.

11. Sylvia Nasar "Fed Gives New Evidence of 80's Gains by Richest," *New York Times*, April 21, 1992, p. 1.

12. Edsall, *Chain Reaction*, p. 196.

13. Bartlett and Steele, "How the Game was Rigged Against the Middle Class," p. 16A.

14. Donald L. Bartlett and James B. Steele, "Big Business Hits the Jackpot with Billions in Tax Breaks," *Philadelphia Inquirer*, October 22, 1991, p. 18A.

15. Edsall, *Chain Reaction*, p. 193.

16. Bartlett and Steele, "Big Business Hits the Jackpot with Billions in Tax Breaks," p. 18A.

17. Stanley Meisler and Sam Fulwood III, "Economic Gap Bodes Ill for U.S.," *Los Angeles Times*, July 15, 1990, p. A1. Robert Pear, "Ranks of U.S. Poor Reach 35.7 Million, The Most Since '64," *New York Times*, September 4, 1992, p. 1. Guy Gugliotta, "Number of Poor Americans Rises for 3rd Year," *Washington Post*, October 5, 1993, p. A6.

18. Spencer Rich, "Low-Paying Jobs Up Sharply in Decade, U.S. Says," *Washington Post*, May 12, 1992, p. A7. Spencer Rich, "U.S. Poverty Rate Up; Median Income Falls," *Washington Post*, September 27, 1991, pp. A1, A13.

19. Paul Taylor, "Study Finds Financial Chasm Between 2 Generations of Families," *Washington Post*, April 15, 1992, p. A3.

20. Spencer Rich, "Millions More Using Food Stamps Amid Recession," *Washington Post*, May 24, 1992, p. A1. Jason DeParle, "Food Stamp Users Up Sharply in Sign of Weak Recovery," *New York Times*, March 2, 1993, p. 1.

21. Lawrence Mishel and Jared Bernstein, "Job Destruction: Worse Than We Thought," *Challenge*, September/October 1992, pp. 6–7. Meisler and Fulwood, "Economic Gap Bodes Ill for U.S.," p. A1. Bartlett and Steele, "How the Game was Rigged Against the Middle Class," p. 18A.

22. Fox Butterfield, "New England's Siren Call of 80's Becomes Echo of the Depression," *New York Times*, December 13, 1991, pp. 1, 30.

23. Sylvia Nasar, "Employment in Service Industry, Engine for Boom of 80's, Falters," *New York Times*, January 2, 1992, p. 1. Bartlett and Steele, "How the Game was Rigged Against the Middle Class," p. 18A. According to Kevin Phillips, the "contingent" labor force doubled to approximately 25 percent of the total work population between 1980 and 1987. Phillips, *The Politics of Rich and Poor*, p. 21.

24. Peter Kilborn, "New Jobs Lack the Old Security in a Time of 'Disposable Workers'," *New York Times*, March 15, 1993, pp. 1, 15. Clare Ansberry, "Workers Are Forced to Take More Jobs with Few Benefits," *Wall Street Journal*, March 11, 1993, p. 1.

25. Mark Feinberg, "Warning: Work is Hazardous to Your Health," *The Progressive* (January 1992): 26. "U.S. Job Death Rate Still Relatively High," *New York Times*, September 1, 1988, p. 8. *Binghamton Press and Sun Bulletin*, October 23, 1989, p. 10. Doug Henwood, "Recovery? Not by a Long Shot," *The Nation*, September 9, 1991, p. 263. Allen Freedman, "Workers Stiffed," *The Washington Monthly*, November 1992, pp. 25.

26. Freedman, "Workers Stiffed," p. 26.

27. Mary Lee Kerr and Bob Hall, "Chickens Come Home to Roost," *The Progressive* (January 1992): 29.

28. *Philadelphia Inquirer*, September 8, 1991, p. 8A.

29. Quoted in Kerr and Hall, "Chickens Come Home to Roost," p. 29.

30. See Gina Kolata, "More Children Are Employed, Often Perilously," *New York Times*, June 21, 1992, pp. 1, 22. Also see U.S. General Accounting Office, *Child Labor: Increase in Detected Child Labor Violations Throughout the United States*, HRD–90–116, April 30, 1990.

31. Quoted in "U.S. Job Death Rate Still Relatively High," p. 8.

32. Feinberg, "Warning: Work is Hazardous to Your Health," p. 28. L. Stuart Ditzen, "Bureaucracy Holding Up Workplace-Safety Rules," *Philadelphia Inquirer*, September 18, 1992, p. A13.

33. *Binghamton Press and Sun Bulletin*, October 23, 1989, p. 10. Ditzen, "Bureaucracy Holding Up Workplace-Safety Rules," p. A13.

34. Calvin Sims, "Building Jobs Underpaid, Officials Say," *New York Times*, February 18, 1992, p. B1.

35. See Jason DeParle, "House Data on Income Sets Off Debate on Fairness in America," *New York Times*, May 22, 1992, p. 16.

36. Juliet B. Schor, *The Overworked American: The Unexpected Decline of Leisure* (New York: Basic Books, 1991), p. 29. David M. Gordon, "It

Works Out That Americans Spend More, Not Less, Time on the Job," *Los Angeles Times*, February 23, 1992, p. D2.

37. Schor, *The Overworked American*, p. 33 (author's emphasis). Most European countries give their workers more than twice the number of paid vacation days annually than what American workers receive. See Laura Leete-Guy and Juliet B. Short, *The Great American Time Squeeze*, Briefing Paper, Economic Policy Institute, Washington, D.C. February 1992, pp. 18–19.

38. Jerry Moskal, "Study: Family Evolves in U.S. After Economy," *Binghamton Press and Sun Bulletin*, September 21, 1989, p. 6.

39. Quoted in Robert Pear, "Poverty Termed a Divorce Factor," *New York Times*, January 19, 1993, p. 10. Also see "Love & Money," *Business Week*, October 19, 1992, p. 58.

40. *Philadelphia Inquirer*, August 9, 1989.

41. Wolff, "Walking Small at Munich," p. C8. "Why We Should Invest in Human Capital," *Business Week*, December 17, 1990, p. 89.

42. Seth Mydans, "For Skilled Foreigners, Lower Hurdles to U.S.," *New York Times*, November 5, 1990, p. 12.

43. J. C. Barden, "Lower Mortality Rate Masks Lag on Infant Health," *New York Times*, September 2, 1991, p. 9.

44. E. J. Dionne Jr., "Speeches, Statistics and Some Unsettling Facts About America's Changed Prospects," *Washington Post*, October 16, 1991, p. A1. Patrice Gaines-Carter, "Project Delivers Healthy Babies," *Washington Post*, October 16, 1991, p. A1.

45. Susan Faludi, *Backlash: The Undeclared War Against American Women* (New York: Crown Publishers, 1991), p. 428.

46. Susan Chira, "Poverty's Toll on Health is Plague of U.S. Schools," *New York Times*, October 5, 1991, p. 1.

47. Faludi, *Backlash*, p. 428.

48. See Robert Pear, "19 Cities Listed for Aid to Cut Infant Mortality," *New York Times*, March 8, 1991, p. 12. *Binghamton Press and Sun Bulletin*, September 29, 1991, p. 1.

49. See Spencer Rich, "Report Card on Youth: Downward Trends Dominate," *Washington Post*, March 24, 1992, p. A17. Paul Taylor, "Report Notes 30-Year Decline in Well-Being of U.S. Children," *Washington Post*, January 3, 1991, p. A9.

50. Dionne, "Speeches, Statistics and Some Unsettling Facts About America's Changed Prospects," p. C3.

51. Barbara Vobejda, "Child Poverty Rate Rose During Prosperous '80s," *Washington Post*, July 8, 1992, p. A3. Also see "Behind Jobless Figures, A Rise in Poor Children," *New York Times*, November 26, 1991, p. 6.

52. See Paul Taylor, "Survey Faults Private Health Coverage," *Washington Post*, January 8, 1992, p. A5.

53. *Washington Post*, October 2, 1989, p. A4.

54. See Chira, "Poverty's Toll on Health is Plague of U.S. Schools," p. 6.

55. Robert Pear, "Poverty in U.S. Grew Faster Than Population Last Year," *New York Times*, October 5, 1993, p. 20.

56. See Warren E. Leary, "Gloomy Report on the Health of Teen-Agers," *New York Times*, June 9, 1990, p. 24.

57. Quoted in Tamar Lewin, "Nursing Homes Rethink Tying Aged as Protection," *New York Times*, December 28, 1989, p. B10.

58. Ibid.

59. Quoted in James Bennet, "Hidden Malnutrition Worsens Health of Elderly," *New York Times*, October 10, 1992, p. 27.

60. See Philip J. Hilts, "U.S. Returns to 1820s in Care of Mentally Ill, Study Asserts," *New York Times*, September 12, 1990, p. 28.

61. Quoted in Michael Specter, "Neglected for Years, TB is Back With Strains That Are Deadlier," *New York Times*, October 11, 1992, pp. 1, 44.

62. See Mireya Navarro, "TB Cases Rose by 38% in '90 For New York," *New York Times*, March 21, 1991, pp. 25, 27. *Chicago Sun-Times*, March 3, 1991, p. 75.

63. Robert Pear, "Fewer Now Have Health Insurance," *New York Times*, December 15, 1993, p. 24.

64. Donald L. Bartlett and James B. Steele, "For Millions in U.S., a Harsh Reality: It's Not Safe to Get Sick," *Philadelphia Inquirer*, October 25, 1991, pp. 1A, 20A. Susan Dentzer, "Scandalous Health Care," *U.S. News & World Report*, March 12, 1990, p. 25. Spencer Rich, "Number Lacking Health Insurance Grown," *Washington Post*, February 29, 1992, p. A10.

65. Dentzer, "Scandalous Health Care," p. 25. Also see Glenn Kramon, "Small Business Is Overwhelmed by Health Costs," *New York Times*, October 1, 1989, pp. 1, 30.

66. Donald L. Bartlett and James B. Steele, "The Lucrative Business of Bankruptcy," *Philadelphia Inquirer*, October 21, 1991, p. 12A. "Bankruptcy Filings Rise 21% to Set Record in 1991," *Washington Post*, March 3, 1992, p. D1.

67. Bartlett and Steele, "For Millions in U.S., a Harsh Reality: It's Not Safe to Get Sick," p. 20A.

68. Statement by William J. Hughes, Chairman, Subcommittee on Retirement Income and Employment, in U.S. House, Joint Hearing Select Committee on Ageing and the Subcommittee on Investment, Jobs, and Prices of the Joint Economic Committee, *Using Public Pensions to Balance State and Local Budgets: The Impact on Public Employees, Retirees, and Taxpayers*, 102nd Congress, 1st Session, November 20, 1991 (Washington, D.C., U.S. Government Printing Office, 1992), p. 12.

69. See Milt Freudenheim, "Medical Insurance is Being Cut Back for Many Retirees," *New York Times*, June 28, 1992, pp. 1, 20.

70. Milt Freudenheim, "Companies Acting to Trim Benefits Promised Retirees," *New York Times*, December 24, 1992, p. 1.

71. Michael Abramowitz, "The Urban Boom: Who Benefits?" *Washington Post*, May 10, 1992, p. H4. Barbara Vobejda, "Urban Recovery Impeded by Changes of Past Three Decades," *Washington Post*, May 8, 1992, p. A11.

72. Barbara Vobejda, "Mayors' Pleas Take on a New-Found Urgency," *Washington Post*, May 16, 1992, p. A8. Robert Suro, "Mayors in Both Parties Voice Frustration," *New York Times*, June 21, 1992, p. 22.

73. Demetrios Caraley, "Washington Abandons the Cities," *Political Science Quarterly* 107, no. 1 (Spring 1992): 8.

74. Abramowitz, "The Urban Boom: Who Benefits?" p. A8.

75. "Rebuilding America: The Mind-Numbing Cost," *Business Week* (Special Issue 'Reinventing America') 1992, pp. 196–97. Also see Faux and Schafer, *Increasing Public Investment*, pp. 6, 10.

76. "The Cities," *Congressional Research Service Review* (November–December 1988).

77. Barbara Vobejda, "Children's Poverty Rose in '80s," *Washington Post*, August 12, 1992, p. A3.

78. See Spencer Rich, "Dispelling Myths About Where America's Homeless People Come From," *Washington Post*, December 4, 1991, p. A23. Celia W. Dugger, "Study Finds Vast Undercount of New York City Homeless," *New York Times*, November 16, 1993, pp. 1, B4.

79. Quoted in "The Cities."

80. See Rich, "Dispelling Myths About Where America's Homeless People Come From," p. A23. Michael Winerip, "Refusing to Overlook the Homeless," *New York Times*, November 15, 1992, p. 41.

81. *Christian Science Monitor* (International Weekly Edition), October 5–11, 1989, p. 1. U.S. Congress, House, Committee on Banking, Finance and Urban Affairs, *Economic Distress in Our Cities*, Chairman's Report, 102nd Congress, 2nd Session, Committee Print 102-12, April 1992 (Washington, D.C.: U.S. Government Printing Office, 1992), p. 11.

82. Jason DeParle, "Private Interests Are Said to Benefit From U.S. Plan for Needy," *New York Times*, March 18, 1992, p. 16.

83. See *Philadelphia Inquirer*, August 9, 1989. Lynn Ludlow, "Doors Foreclosing on American Dream," *San Francisco Examiner*, August 2, 1992, p. E1. Nick Ravo, "Surge in Home Foreclosures and Evictions Shattering Families," *New York Times*, November 15, 1992, p. 41.

84. *Christian Science Monitor* (International Weekly Edition), October 5–11, 1989, p. 1.

85. See James Petras and Christian Davenport, "Crime and the Transformation of Capitalism," *Crime, Law and Social Change* 16 (1991): 155–75.

86. Mary Merva and Richard Fowles, *Effects of Diminished Economic*

Opportunities on Social Stress, Briefing Paper, Economic Policy Institute, Washington, D.C., October 1992, pp. 11–12.

87. Elizabeth Kolbert, "Criminal Justice: Priority Proves Elusive for Cuomo," *New York Times*, October 2, 1990, p. B1.

88. Patricia Horn, "Caging America," *Dollars & Sense* 169 (September 1991): 13. The statistical data is taken from the Corrections Compendium.

89. See Fox Butterfield, "U.S. Expands Its Lead in Rate of Imprisonment," *New York Times*, February 11, 1992, p. 16.

90. See Jason DeParle, "Young Black Men in Capital: Study Finds 42% in Courts," *New York Times*, April 18, 1992, p. 1.

91. See Robert Suro, "Crime and Its Amplified Echoes Are Rearranging People's Lives," *New York Times*, February 9, 1992, p. E1. Dionne, Jr., "Speeches, Statistics and Some Unsettling Facts About America's Changed Prospects," p. C3. Michael Isikoff, "D.C. Area Isn't Alone in Epidemic of Killing," *Washington Post*, December 16, 1991, p. A21. "Many Cities Setting Records for Homicides in Year," *New York Times*, December 9, 1990, p. 41. U.S. Congress, Senate Judiciary Committee and the International Narcotics Control Caucus, *The President's Drug Strategy: Has it Worked?* Report prepared by the Majority Staffs, September 1992, p. 22.

92. See George Winslow, "A System Out of Control, Not Just One Bank," *In These Times* (October 23–29, 1991): 8. George Winslow, "New Capitalism: Bank Fraud, Drug Trade, Espionage," *In These Times* (October 30–November 5, 1991): 9. For an extended discussion of BCCI and its involvement with the U.S. banking community, see Mark Potts, et al., *Dirty Money* (Washington, D.C.: National Press Books, 1992).

93. Stephen Labaton, "Banking's Technology Helps Drug Dealers Export Cash. . . . ," *New York Times*, August 14, 1989, pp. 1, B4.

94. W. John Moore, "Nixing the Cash Injection," *National Journal*, December 2, 1989, pp. 2924–25.

95. Ibid., p. 2928.

96. Quoted in Labaton, "Banking's Technology Helps Drug Dealers Export Cash. . . . ," p. 1.

97. U.S. Congress, *The President's Drug Strategy: Has it Worked?* pp. 1, 3.

98. See Arms Control and Foreign Policy Caucus, *The Developing World: Danger Point for U.S. Security* (Washington, D.C.: U.S. Congress, House, August 1, 1989), p. 68.

99. William Kornblum, Director of the Center for Social Research, City University of New York, quoted in Stephen Labaton, "The Cost of Drug Abuse: $60 Billion a Year," *New York Times*, December 5, 1989, p. D6. U.S. Congress, *The President's Drug Strategy: Has it Worked?* p. ii.

100. Ibid.

101. William Glaberson, "Mean Streets Force New Yorkers to Just Walk on By," *New York Times*, February 19, 1990, p. B2.

102. Matthew Cooper, "The Rich in America," *U.S. News & World*

Report, November 18, 1991, p. 36. Also see "Government by the Nice for the Nice," *The Economist*, July 25, 1992, pp. 29–30.

103. Donald L. Bartlett and James B. Steele, "The High Cost of Deregulation: Joblessness, Bankruptcy, Debt," *Philadelphia Inquirer*, October 24, 1991, pp. 1A, 20A. Bartlett and Steele, "The Lucrative Business of Bankruptcy," p. 12A.

104. "Is Your Job Safe?" *U.S. News & World Report*, January 13, 1992, p. 44.

105. Sarah Bartlett, "Job Losses in New York Region Erode 80's Growth," *New York Times*, December 20, 1991, p. 1.

106. See Louis Uchitelle, "The Undercounted Unemployed," *New York Times*, January 8, 1992, pp. D1, D4. "Is Your Job Safe?" pp. 44–45. Robert D. Hershey, Jr., "Jobless Rate Jumps to 7.8%, Raising Doubts on Recovery," *New York Times*, July 3, 1992, p. 12.

107. See "Is Your Job Safe?," pp. 45, 48. Warren Brown, "GM Loses Record $4.5 Billion, Announces 12 Plant Closings," *Washington Post*, February 25, 1992, p. A1. Allen R. Myerson, "Amoco Is Cutting 8,500 Jobs," *New York Times*, July 9, 1992, p. D1. Felicity Barringer, "Laid-Off Bosses Scramble in a Changing World," *New York Times*, July 12, 1992, p. 6E. Steven Greenhouse, "Income Data Show Years of Erosion for U.S. Workers," *New York Times*, September 7, 1992. Steve Lohr, "Big Companies Cloud Recovery by Cutting Jobs," *New York Times*, December 17, 1992 p. 1. Allen R. Myerson, "I.B.M. To Eliminate 25,000 Jobs in 1993 and Shut Plants," *New York Times*, December 16, 1992, pp.1,D4.

108. See Steven Prokesch, "Job Rate Hits a 25-Year Record in New York City," *New York Times*, February 6, 1993, p. 1. Kara Swisher, "Sears Cut 50,000 Jobs in Shake-Up," *Washington Post*, January 26, 1993, p. A10. Louis Uchitelle, "3 Aircraft Companies Announce Big Job Cutbacks as Orders Fall," *New York Times*, January 27, 1993, p. 1. Steven Pearlstein, "A Wave of Change Sweeps U.S. Firms," *Washington Post*, January 27, 1993, pp. 1, 9.

109. Thomas K. Luech, "Though End of Recession is Here, Prosperity Isn't Even Near Corner," *New York Times*, January 10, 1993, p. 32.

110. "Jobs," *Business Week*, February 22, 1993, p. 68.

111. *Philadelphia Inquirer*, January 4, 1991, p. 11A.

112. Edsall, *Chain Reaction*, pp. 162, 192.

113. *Philadelphia Inquirer*, August 9, 1989.

114. Jason DeParle, "Fueled by Social Trends, Welfare Cases Are Rising," *New York Times*, January 19, 1992, p. 16. Paul Taylor, "Survey Finds Many State Cuts Aimed at Poorest of Poor," *Washington Post*, December 19, 1991. p. A23. Robert Pear, "Poverty in U.S. Grew Faster Than Population Last Year," p. 20.

115. See Robin Toner, "Politics of Welfare: Focusing on the Problems," *New York Times*, July 5, 1992, p. 16.

116. Robert Pear, "Many States Cut Food Allotments for Poor Families," *New York Times*, May 29, 1990, pp. 1, 16.

117. Donald L. Bartlett and James B. Steele, "When You Retire, Will There Be a Pension Waiting?" *Philadelphia Inquirer*, October 27, 1991, pp. 1A, 16A. Sylvia Nasar, "Pensions Covering Lower Percentage of U.S. Work Force," *New York Times*, April 13, 1992, p. 1.

118. Louis Uchitelle, "Company-Financed Pensions Are Failing to Fulfill Promise," *New York Times*, May 29, 1990, pp. 1, D5.

119. Bartlett and Steele, "When You Retire, Will There Be a Pension Waiting?," p. 16A.

120. Ibid., p. 1A.

121. Jeff Gerth, "U.S. Pension Agency is in Deep Trouble, Economists Warn," *New York Times*, December 20, 1992, p. 1. Also see David A. Vise, "Federal Survey Finds Pension's Problems Growing," *Washington Post*, November 20, 1992, p. F1. David A. Vise, "Government Has Massive Pension Fund Shortfall," *Washington Post*, November 22, 1993, p. A1. David A. Vise, "Going After the Pension Gaps," *Washington Post*, November 23, 1993, p. C1.

122. Alan Deutschman, "The Great Pension Robbery," *Fortune*, January 13, 1992, p. 76.

123. *Philadelphia Inquirer*, December 31, 1989, p. 3A.

124. See "Is Your Job Safe?" p. 48. Uchitelle, "The Undercounted Unemployed," p. D4.

125. See Linda Grant, "Recipe for Survival," *Los Angeles Times*, May 31, 1992, pp. D1, D3.

126. "Is Your Job Safe?" p. 48.

127. Sylvia Nasar, "Unexplored Territory: A Recession in Services," *New York Times*, February 3, 1991, p. 26.

128. Robert D. Hershey, "U.S. Trade In Services At a Deficit," *New York Times*, September 13, 1989, p. D22.

129. See, for example, Ronald Radosh, *American Labor and United States Foreign Policy* (New York: Random House, 1969).

130. Edsall, *Chain Reaction*, p. 194. David Brody, "The Breakdown of Labor's Social Contract," *Dissent* (Winter 1992): 33. Diane Alters, "Number of Union Jobs Declines Precipitously," *San Francisco Examiner*, April 19, 1992, p. E4.

131. Frank Swoboda, "Labor Loses the Strike As a Weapon," *Washington Post*, July 5, 1992, p. H1.

132. John Holusha, "Unions Are Expanding Their Role to Survive in the 90's," *New York Times*, August 19, 1990, p. 12F.

133. Ibid..

134. Quoted in Frank Swoboda, "The Bitter Harvest of a Global Shift," *Washington Post*, April 19, 1992, p. H5. Also see David Moberg, "Union Busting, Past and Present," *Dissent* (Winter 1992): 79. Martin Walker, "No Arresting the Sad Decline of Organized Labor," *Guardian Weekly*, April 26, 1992, p. 10. Steven Greenhouse, "The Union Movement Loses Another Big One," *New York Times*, April 19, 1992. p. E2.

135. Holusha, "Unions Are Expanding Their Role to Survive in the 90's," p. 12F.

136. Moberg, "Union Busting, Past and Present," p. 77.

137. Philip Shenon, "Voter Turnout Still Poor, With 3 Exceptions," *New York Times*, November 11, 1990, p. 27. George Graham, "Half of America Turns to the Apathy Party," *Financial Times*, April 15, 1992, p. 6. Paul Taylor, *See How They Run: Electing the President in an Age of Mediaocracy* (New York: Alfred A. Knopf, 1990), P. 241; U.S. Department of Commerce, *Statistical Abstract of the United States 1993* (Washington, D.C.: U.S. Government Printing Office, 1993), p. 284.

138. E. J. Dionne, Jr., *Why Americans Hate Politics* (New York: Simon & Schuster, 1991), pp. 316–17.

139. Quoted in Dan Balz and Richard Morin, "A Tide of Pessimism and Political Powerlessness Arises," *Washington Post*, November 3, 1991, p. A16.

140. Quoted in Michael Oreskes, "American Politics Loses Way As Polls Displace Leadership," *New York Times*, March 18, 1990, p. 22.

141. Ibid. Michael Wines, "Candidates for Congress Spent Record $678 Million, a 52% Jump" *New York Times*, March 5, 1993, p. 12.

142. Charles B. Babcock, "$100,000 Political Donations on the Rise Again," *Washington Post*, September 30, 1991, p. A4. Carol Matlack, " 'Soft' Rain Still Falling," *National Journal*, February 29, 1992, pp. 520–21. Stephen Labaton, "Where the 'Soft Money' Comes From," *New York Times*, July 10, 1992, p. 18. Peter H. Stone, "Return of the Fat Cats," *National Journal*, October 17, 1992, p. 2351. Linda Feldmann, "Give Money and They Call Back," *Christian Science Monitor*, November 3, 1992, p. 3.

143. Stone, "Return of the Fat Cats," p. 2352. Barbara Demick, "Campaign Financing Thrives on Loopholes," *Philadelphia Inquirer*, October 25, 1992, p. A10.

144. Neil A. Lewis, "Exemption is Allowing Big Spenders to Skirt Curbs on Aid to Candidates," *New York Times*, May 16, 1992, p. 7. Sara Fritz, James Risen, and Dwight Morris, "A Winning Strategy on Tax Breaks," *Los Angeles Times*, March 15, 1992, p. A12.

145. Quoted in Balz and Morin, "A Tide of Pessimism and Political Powerlessness Arises," p. A16.

146. See Robin Toner, "Turned Off by Campaigns, Or Just Too Busy to Vote," *New York Times*, November 7, 1990, p. B6.

147. Quoted in Ibid..

148. Quoted in Martin Walker, "Price Tag for Inner-City Renewal Adds to Budget Deficit," *Guardian Weekly*, May 24, 1992, p. 8. Also see Balz and Morin, "A Tide of Pessimism and Political Powerlessness Arises," pp. A1, A16.

149. Quoted in Richard Morin and E. J. Dionne, Jr., "Majority of Voters Say Parties Have Lost Touch," *Washington Post*, July 8, 1992, p. A10.

150. Eighty-two percent of Americans responded positively to this statement in a 1992 Gallup Poll. See *The Gallup Poll Monthly* 316 (January 1992): 13.

4. EPILOGUE: THE CLINTON ADMINISTRATION: GLOBAL LEADERSHIP VS. DOMESTIC RECOVERY

1. "U.S. Launches $4bn Fund to Aid Russian Privatization," *Financial Times*, April 15, 1993, p. 1.

2. Quoted in David E. Rosenbaum, "Clinton Leads Experts in Discussion on Economy," *New York Times*, December 15, 1992, p. 1.

3. Quoted in Thomas L. Friedman, "Congress Listens, Waiting to See If the Plan Sells," *New York Times*, February 18, 1993, p. 16.

4. Quoted in Keith Bradsher, "Top Economic Aide Tells Clients to Keep in Touch," *New York Times*, February 5, 1993, pp. 1, 16.

5. Quoted in David S. Hilzenrath, "Business Basks in Bentsen's Selection for Treasury," *Washington Post*, December 8, 1992, p. A1.

6. Jamie Stiehm, "If You're Clever—And Very Rich," *The Nation*, October 18, 1993, p. 422.

7. Peter H. Stone, "Clinton Gives Realtors a Big Break," *National Journal*, February 27, 1993, p. 526.

8. John H. Cushman, Jr., "Wealthy to be able to Spread Out Pain of '93 Tax Increase," *New York Times*, August 5, 1993, p. 1.

9. Quoted in Steven Greenhouse, "Administration Completing Plan to Ease Rules on Bank Lending," *New York Times*, February 24, 1993, pp. 1, D2.

10. Quoted Steven Pearlstein, "Clinton Advisers Still Stress New Economic Tack," *Washington Post*, December 9, 1992, p. A14.

11. David M. Gordon, "The Upsides and the Downsides," *The Nation*, March 15, 1993, p. 344.

12. Martin Tolchin, "Privatizing Urged to Improve Roads," *New York Times*, October 1, 1993, p. 12.

13. Todd Schaefer, *Still Neglecting Public Investment*, Briefing Paper, Economic Policy Institute, Washington, D.C., September 1993, p. 1.

14. "An Uphill Struggle," *U.S. News & World Report*, November 8, 1993, p. 64.

15. Thomas L. Friedman, "Clinton Supports Creating Fund Designated Solely to Cut Deficit," *New York Times*, May 13, 1993, p. 1.

16. See Amy Kaslow, "Clinton's Job Plan: Ready! Train! Wait!" *Christian Science Monitor* (International Weekly Edition), March 26–April 1, 1993, p. 4.

17. "Roaring Back," *Los Angeles Times*, September 5, 1993, p. D4. John Dillon, "U.S. Work Force Hit Hard As Manufacturing Jobs Flee," *Christian Science Monitor*, October 7, 1993, p. 4. "The Party's Not Over Yet," *Business Week*, January 10, 1994, p. 83.

18. Louis Uchitelle, "Fewer Jobs Filled As Factories Rely on Overtime Pay," *New York Times*, May 16, 1993, p. 1.

19. See Doug Henwood, "Happy Days Again," *The Nation*, February 21, 1994, p. 221. John Miller, "As the Economy Expands, Opportunity Contracts," *Dollars & Sense*, May/June 1994, pp. 9–10. "U.S. Work Force Hit Hard as Manufacturing Jobs Flee," p. 4. Steven Pearlstein, "Layoffs Become a Lasting Reality," *Washington Post*, November 6, 1993, p. A10. John Holusha, "10,000 Jobs to be Cut by Kodak," *New York Times*, August 19, 1993, p. D1. Steve Lohr, "More Cuts by 2 Big Companies," *New York Times*, November 25, 1993, p. D1.

20. Louis Uchitelle, "More Are Forced into Ranks of Self-Employed at Low Pay," *New York Times*, November 15, 1993, pp. 1, D2. Bob Herbert, "America's Job Disaster, *New York Times*, December 1, 1993, p. 23.

21. "Economic Trends," *Business Week*, September 27, 1993, p. 28.

22. Ibid.

23. "Economic Trends," p. 28. Also see Paul Starobin, "Unequal Shares," *National Journal*, September 11, 1993, p. 2177.

24. Tony Horwitz, "The Working Poor: Minimum Wage Jobs Give Many Americans Only a Miserable Life," *Wall Street Journal*, November 12, 1993, p. 1.

25. "Homeless Families Increase in Cities," *New York Times*, December 22, 1993, p. 18.

26. Quoted in Mark Jaffe, "Even With Reform, Money Talks," *Philadelphia Inquirer*, September 21, 1993, p. A10.

27. Eric Schmitt, "$261 Billion Set for the Military," *New York Times*, November 7, 1993, p. 25.

28. Michael R. Gordon, "Pentagon's Budget Gap Is Narrowed to $31 Billion," *New York Times*, December 18, 1993, p. 8. Also see Michael R. Gordon, "Pentagon Fights Budget Officials Over $50 Billion," *New York Times*, December 10, 1993, pp. 1, 28.

29. See Eric Schmitt, "Pentagon Nominee Strives For Global Strategist Role," *New York Times*, February 3, 1994, p. 9.

30. Martin Walker, "Crime Bill with a Racial Bite," *Guardian Weekly*, May 1, 1994, p. 6. Paulette Thomas, "Making Crime Pay: Triangle of Interests Creates Infrastructure to Fight Lawlessness," *Wall Street Journal*, May 12, 1994, p. 1.

31. Quoted in John M. Goshko and Don Oberdorfer, "U.S. to Study Wider Options on Balkans," *Washington Post*, January 28, 1993, p. A16.

32. Quoted in Martin Walker, "Budget Cut—Punches Pulled?" *Guardian Weekly*, July 4, 1993, p. 7.

33. See Douglas Jehl, "Campaign is Begun to Protect Money For Spy Agencies," *New York Times*, March 14, 1993, pp. 1, 28. Douglas Jehl, "Clinton Seeking More Money for Spying, Aides Say," *New York Times*, April 15, 1993, pp. 1, 16.

34. Anthony Lake, "From Containment to Enlargement," address at

Johns Hopkins University, Washington, D.C., September 21, 1993, reprinted in U.S. Department of State, *Dispatch*, September 27, 1993, pp. 658–664.

35. Warren Christopher, "Nato and US Foreign Policy," excerpts from an address at NATO Headquarters, Brussels, February 26, 1993, reprinted in U.S. Department of State. *Dispatch*, March 1, 1993, p. 120.

36. Warren Christopher, quoted in Daniel Williams and Ann Devroy, "U.S. Bombing, Credibility Linked," *Washington Post*, April 22, 1994, p. A1. Also see Douglas Jehl, "Clinton Urging NATO Attacks to Deter Serbs," *New York Times*, April 21, 1994, p. 1. Martin Walker, "Nato Becomes an Enforcer," *Guardian Weekly*, February 20, 1994, p. 5.

37. Warren Christopher, quoted in "Iraq Provides Timely Focus As Nominee Faces Panel," *Congressional Quarterly Weekly Report*, January 16, 1993, p. 136.

38. Bill Clinton, quoted in *CubaINFO*, December 17, 1993, p. 1.

39. Warren Christopher, "Supporting U.S. Business in Asia and Around the World," speech to the American Business Council, Singapore, July 27, 1993, reprinted in U.S. Department of State, *Dispatch*, August 2, 1993, p. 551.

40. "Clinton Decides: Let the Exports Flow," *Business Week*, October 11, 1993, p. 51. Also see "Greasing the Skids for Exports," *Business Week*, January 31, 1994, pp. 66–67.

41. Keith Bradsher, "U.S. to Aid Industry in Computer Battle With the Japanese," *New York Times*, April 27, 1994, pp. 1, D5. Also see Edmund L. Andrews, "Washington Growing as a Financial Angel to Industry," *New York Times*, May 1, 1994, p. F3.

42. Secretary of State Warren Christopher, quoted in John Lyons, "US, Japan Trade Talks Deadlocked," *The Australian*, February 12–13, 1993, p. 13. Also see Andrew Pollack, "U.S. Steps Up the Pressure in Tokyo," *New York Times*, April 24, 1993, pp. 37, 38.

43. "Region's Capital Inflow Rise," *Latin American Monitor: Southern Cone* (May 1993): 1144.

44. Valerie Reitman, "U.S. Firms Turn to the Developing World," *Wall Street Journal*, August 4, 1993, p. 2. Patrick Tyler, "Economic Focus in Shanghai: Catching Up," *New York Times*, December 22, 1993, p. 8.

45. Quoted in "NAFTA: Let's Make a Deal," *Business Week*, November 8, 1993, p. 32.

46. See Jerome I. Levinson, *The Labor Side Accord to the North American Free Trade Agreement*, Briefing Paper, Economic Policy Institute, Washington, D.C., September 1993, p. 9.

47. Ibid., p. 6.

48. Anthony DePalma, "Law Protects Mexico's Workers But its Enforcement is Often Lax," *New York Times*, August 15, 1993, p. 1.

49. Tim Golden, "A History of Pollution in Mexico Casts Clouds Over Trade Accord," *New York Times*, August 16, 1993, p. 7.

50. "Why NAFTA Just Might Squeak Through," *Business Week*, August 30, 1993, p. 36. U.S. General Accounting Office, *U.S.-Mexico Trade: The Maquiladora Industry and U.S. Employment*, B-253952, July 1993, p. 3.

51. Stanley C. Gault, Chairman, Goodyear Tire & Rubber Company, quoted in "Why NAFTA Just Might Squeak Through," p. 36.

52. Jerome I. Levinson, a former general counsel of the Inter-American Development Bank, quoted in Tim McCarthy, "NAFTA Called Big Corporate Power Play," *National Catholic Reporter*, November 19, 1993, pp. 14–15.

53. Thomas L. Friedman, "Bright Sun of Trade Rising in the East," *New York Times*, November 19, 1993, p. 6.

54. "This Isn't Your Usual Clinton Gabfest," *Business Week*, November 15, 1993, p. 52.

55. See "Japanese Manufacturing: Asian Promise," *The Economist*, June 12, 1993, pp. 72–73. Philip Shenon, "Missing Out on a Glittering Market," *New York Times*, September 12, 1993, pp. F1, F6.

56. See Keith Bradsher, "Relying on the Irresistible Force of GATT's Appeal," *New York Times*, December 13, 1993, pp. D1, D5.

57. "Gatt: Who Wins What," *Guardian Weekly*, December 26, 1993, p. 6.

58. Quoted in Martin Walker, "Clinton Forced into Damage Limitation," *Guardian Weekly*, October 17, 1993, p. 6.

59. See Elaine Sciolino, "U.S. Is Abandoning 'Shock Therapy' for the Russians," *New York Times*, December 21, 1993, pp. 1, 14. George Graham, "IMF Will Not Ease Stance on Moscow Cash Aid," *Financial Times*, January 7, 1994, p. 1.

60. Quoted in Steven Greenhouse, "U.S. Issues a Warning to Russia To Keep Economic Reform Going," *New York Times*, January 25, 1994, p. 1.

61. Bill Clinton, "American Leadership and Global Change," address at American University, Washington, D.C., February 26, 1993, in U.S. Department of State, *Dispatch*, March 1, 1993, p. 115.

62. See Steve Coll and Douglas Farah, "Panama Still a Conduit for Cocaine Profits," *Washington Post*, September 20, 1993, pp. A1, A14.

63. Michael R. Gordon with John H. Cushman, Jr., "U.S. Supported Hunt for Aidid; Now Calls U.N. Policy Skewed," *New York Times*, October 18, 1993, p. 1.

64. See Sciolino, "U.S. Is Abandoning 'Shock Therapy' for the Russians," p. 14.

65. See, for example, David Moberg, "Like Business, Unions Must go Global," *New York Times*, December 19, 1993, p. F13. Robert Bryce, "Mexican Unions Struggle in a Tough Post-NAFTA World," *Christian Science Monitor*, (International Weekly Edition), December 24–30, 1993, p. 7.

66. Jeffrey H. Birnbaum and David Wessel, "Unlikely Allies: President is

Wooing, And Mostly Pleasing, Big-Business Leaders," *Wall Street Journal*, November 19, 1993, p. 1.

CONCLUSION

1. "Transcript of Clinton's First Newspaper Conference at White House," *New York Times*, March 24, 1993, p. 10.